Do you play
STAYMAN?

BY SAMUEL M. STAYMAN

with a foreword by Albert H. Morehead

 ODYSSEY PRESS · NEW YORK

Jacket design and decorations by Frances Giannoni

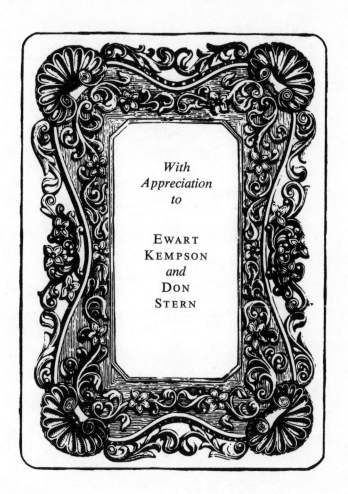

With
Appreciation
to

EWART
KEMPSON
and
DON
STERN

FOREWORD

I ENJOY writing this foreword for the two best reasons in the world—old friendship with the author and great admiration for the book.

Sam Stayman and I emerged from our respective New England colleges at about the same time; we served our apprenticeship in highest-level club bridge in the same clubs against the same players; we have talked out and sometimes fought out bridge theory over as long a period, I am sure, as any two persons in bridge.

It is no accident that Stayman is (and deservedly so) one of the four or five best-known names in bridge throughout the world.

In the history of bridge, there are only a very few instances of great players who are also great theorists. Offhand, I can think of only two or three who can match Stayman's record both in playing successes and in theoretical achievements.

The playing record speaks for itself. Stayman's career includes three consecutive victories in the World Championships. When he left the highest-ranking American team, the new team that he formed immediately defeated his former team and represented the United States in the next World Championship. Since then, he has been official representative of his country in World Championship competition three times.

In the realm of theory, it is generally acknowledged that Sam Stayman knows more about notrump bidding than anyone else. His first two books, both of them on bidding in general but containing much about his notrump methods, were internationally successful. But this new book is the best of them all.

We are in an age of specialization. The great interest in bridge permits specialization; the vast literature of bridge, which has all but exhausted general approaches, demands specialization. Very recently, there have been books devoted solely to the play to the first trick (Fred Karpin), the suit-preference signal (Hy Lavinthal), and many other isolated aspects.

But the most important bid of all, the opening notrump, with its built-in pre-emptive effect combined with maximal transmission of information, had never been fully covered until Stayman wrote this book.

Because of its division into separate sections for the novice and the *cognoscente* and also because of the notable clarity of the presentation, this is a book for every bridge player of every degree of skill. I would venture to say that it is the most important book for most players, because one can profit more by skillful exploitation of the notrump bid than by any other bidding tool vouchsafed to the bridge player.

There also are interludes in the book, always presented in restrained and unheralded fashion, that seem destined to make bridge history. The very concept of the 30-point scale for slam bids based on the coincidence of a distributional fit and no duplication of values must rank in this class.

I have learned a great deal from this book and I am sure every reader will, too.

ALBERT H. MOREHEAD

New York, New York, 1965

CONTENTS

INTRODUCTION

WHAT IS the hypnotic fascination about notrump? Some players are in love with the bid. Many women are deathly afraid of it. The male animal often regards it as his exclusive province. Why?

Partly because a notrump contract is awkward to bid and tricky to play. Declarer at a notrump contract often feels like a sitting target in no-man's land: the enemy can pounce on him from any of four fronts. To manage all four suits without letting one get away is no mean task. Perhaps as reward, a notrump game requires one less trick than the next-ranking major suits. For that reason, notrump is the highroad to scoring game—in fact the axis on which the game of bridge rotates.

Over the years, notrump bidding has been developed to exploit this advantage. Today the opening bid of one notrump is correctly recognized as a solid base from which to probe for the best contract. Bridge experts use it as a stable, limited bid. If a hand truly qualifies for a one-notrump opening, they always make that bid, for it is the most descriptive bid of all. It unfolds almost the whole story of the hand in one shot and steers the partnership toward the best contract.

When the bidding starts with one notrump, there is a comfortable smoothness about the auction. But this very ease should not lull the partnership to a final notrump contract, willy-nilly. Indeed the hands may play better in a major suit. Consider the last time you were in a game contract at notrump with tricks to burn, but the opponents managed to find your weak suit and rake in five tricks before you could bring home your nine. Afterward, you or your partner may have observed that four of a major—or even five of a minor —was on ice.

The simplest example of this is a 4–4 fit in a major suit; it is a bridge axiom that such hands usually play better at four of the major than at three notrump.

But how do you find out if the fit exists? In the old days, you couldn't. When one player opened one notrump and his partner bid two in a major suit, it was anybody's guess whether responder had a 4- or 5-card suit, whether his hand, overall, was anemic or robust. Ironically, the precise opening bid of one notrump had led quickly to a vexing situation.

Fortunately, an ingenious means has been developed to meet the problem. As with most successful concepts, it did not develop overnight. More than twenty years ago, players in Boston, London and elsewhere were experimenting with an artificial two-club bid over an opening notrump to convey various aspects of the hand. In his regular partnerships this writer adapted that two-club bid to ask one precise question, developing a series of responses to convey specific answers to responder. Building upon this base, various bidding sequences were codified, each with its own particular message.

The convention that evolved has since become standard equipment for all classes of players throughout the world. In the Stayman Convention, a two-club response to an opening one-notrump bid asks whether partner has a 4-card major suit and opens up the way to play at a superior major-suit contract when a fit is found. It is worth thousands of points over the year in game-going contracts.

And it is just as profitable for part-score contracts. At last you can stop on a dime in a part-score contract with reasonable assurance that you haven't missed anything and are in the right suit.

Best of all, Stayman is a simple, effective tool that covers a wide range of common situations. Every bid has a logical meaning that is easily understood. Anybody can play the convention and most serious bridge players do; the proof of its efficacy is its widespread adoption throughout the world of bridge.

Stayman helps players *think* their way to the best contract and gets to the heart of bidding values—suit strength, distribution and controls. Stayman encourages teamwork by establishing a network of bids—an integrated system—within which a partnership can function smoothly.

It is most gratifying to note the widespread acceptance of this system since we first codified it about twenty years ago. However, as with any popular movement, Stayman has been distorted and misused, battered and pulled out of shape. It is high time to repair the damage.

Everybody and his cousin are apparently only too happy to "modify" the basic system. Most of these modifications seem rooted in overeagerness. The two-club bid poses a simple question to opener: "Do you have a 4-card major suit?" But the modifiers want to use the same question to inquire about the strength of the notrump opening or to find out at one fell swoop whether opener has *both* majors.

You may wonder what is wrong with this. Isn't is useful to give partner more information rather than less? Not at all. Partner may be totally disinterested, but the opponents will appreciate your thoughtfulness, for it will often direct them to the killing lead and subsequent defense to defeat your final contract.

Responder can fend for himself. If he is truly interested in a further description of opener's hand, he can always ask for it on a later round of bidding.

A successful system has a negative as well as a positive goal. We are all familiar with the positive aim of guiding the partnership to the winning contract. But how many of us pay sufficient heed to the negative goal of keeping the opponents in the dark? A good part of the winning game is to avoid giving aid and comfort to the enemy—and to confuse them, if possible. It is downright naive to give them a clear blueprint of your hand.

The Stayman System as set forth twenty-odd years ago is not inviolate by any means. But the tinkerers we have described are off in the wrong direction. Each bid should tell something about the hand. Gradually bids build up into a bidding *sequence;* then each bid can be sensibly interpreted in the light of the calls that have gone before. Thus a more sharply defined picture of the hand emerges. But this cannot be done with one all-purpose bid without harmful side-effects.

The valid refinements of the Stayman System develop from making these sequences work for us. Aside from the direct message of each bid, there are negative inferences to be drawn. Every time your partner *fails* to bid two clubs over your opening one notrump, you can rule out a host of possible hands with which he would have inquired about your major suits. Similarly when he responds two clubs to your notrump opening, you can eliminate all hands on which he would have made some other bid. Such negative inferences are often more valuable than the direct information you get from any one bid.

By using these sequences logically, we have found when and how to look for minor-suit fits. We also learn early in the auction when it is better to use up the bidding levels and keep the opponents in the dark, or when we need bidding room to probe for our optimum contract.

Perhaps the greatest advantage of the Stayman System is its flexibility. For the average player it should be—and is—simple, direct, easy to remember. On the other hand, the experienced player uses its subtler nuances to keep his expert opponent guessing, while heading for the best contract. Accordingly, this book is divided into two parts, the first for the average player, the second for the more experienced player.

Either way, you'll find it more fun and more rewarding to use this most widely accepted system in a logical way you yourself fully understand.

SAMUEL M. STAYMAN

This book is divided into two parts:

PART ONE
FOR AVERAGE PLAYERS

The basic system—
simple, direct, easy to remember.

PART TWO
FOR ADVANCED PLAYERS

Refinements which provide
for greater accuracy while keeping
the opponents guessing.

A summary of bidding sequences and their meanings
follows each part.

PART ONE

for

AVERAGE
PLAYERS

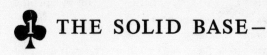 THE SOLID BASE—

THE OPENING BID

OF ONE NOTRUMP

THE OPENING one-notrump bid is limited and precise. Our first task then is to define its limits. Fortunately, the requirements have already been sketched out by a number of popular bridge writers. Still, the outline they have drawn is fuzzy, for bridge writers tend to avoid clear-cut definitions and distinctions. It will pay us to spell out the features promised by this bid, particularly since the soundness of the later bidding rests on this bedrock foundation.

When your partner responds with a Stayman two-club bid, asking further information, you can reply intelligently only if you know the promises you have already made to him by your initial notrump bid. What then can your partner surmise about your strength, distribution and stoppers when he hears you open with one notrump?

First, that your hand counts to 16, 17 or 18 points in high cards—no more, no less.

The valuation is by the standard point-count scale: ace = 4 points, king = 3 points, queen = 2 points, jack = 1 point. In addition, you count 1 distributional point for the fifth card in a suit as good as K J x x. Many authorities assign no points for distribution in valuing a hand for notrump, but clearly an additional card in a usable suit is worth something. Compare these two hands:

(1)   ♠ A 10 3 ♡ A Q   ◇ A K 7 6 2 ♣ 9 5 3

(2)   ♠ A 10 3 ♡ A Q 2 ◇ A K 7 6 ♣ 9 5 3

There is a very good chance that the two of diamonds in (1) will bring home an extra trick in the play; it is only reasonable to recognize that edge by awarding it an extra point.

Secondly, the opening notrump bid promises balanced distribution: 4–3–3–3, 4–4–3–2 or 5–3–3–2.

In the last case, the 5-card suit may be a minor, even a strong one like A K Q 10 8, or it can be a weak major suit like Q x x x x. But with a major suit as good as K J x x x, you will get better results in the long run by opening with one in the major suit rather than with one notrump.

Thirdly, it promises stoppers in three suits.

Since the opening one-notrump bid suggests a game in notrump, it must be prepared to handle the enemy's suit. Thus it requires "stoppers"—holdings that can *stop* the run of the suit the opponents attack by taking a trick in that suit. A stopper consists of an honor card and enough small cards accompanying it so that the honor will not fall prematurely. Here are the weakest stoppers: A, K x, Q x x, J x x x.

SUMMING UP

In sum, then, you open one notrump when you have:

1. 16–18 points, including 1 point for a 5-card suit as good as K J x x x, *and*

2. 4–3–3–3, 4–4–3–2 or 5–3–3–2 distribution (but not if the 5-card suit is a major suit, K J x x x or better) *and*

3. Stoppers in three suits (A, K x, Q x x or J x x x).

Your hand must qualify on all three or else you should find some other call.

RATE YOURSELF

To insure that you have mastered the requirements for an opening one-notrump bid, try yourself on this quiz. Examine the following hands and decide which should be opened with one notrump:

	♠	♡	◇	♣
(1)	A J 4	K 9 3	A K J 2	9 7 3
(2)	A 2	K 7 5	K J 8 5 4	A 5 3
(3)	K J 7 5	A 10	K Q 8 5 3	K 5
(4)	A 6	K 9 8 7	A Q 9	Q 10 7 6
(5)	A 2	K J 10 8 4	K J 5	A J 3
(6)	Q 9 3	A 7	A Q 3	K 8 7 4 2
(7)	A 10 8 4 2	Q J 5	K 4	A Q 2
(8)	9 8 5	A K Q	10 6 5 3	A K J

Answers: Bid one notrump on (1), (2) and (7). The others do not qualify for one reason or another. Regardless of how you scored, you will find it rewarding to check *all* the answers, just to be sure these important principles are firmly implanted.

Explanations:

(1) *Bid one notrump.* You have 16 high-card points: 5 in spades, 3 in hearts, 8 in diamonds, none in clubs; balanced 4–3–3–3 distribution; stoppers in three suits.

(2) *Bid one notrump.* At first, the hand seems to count only 15 points, but you add 1 point for the fifth card in the usable 5-card diamond suit.

(3) *Bid one diamond.* You have enough points, but 5–4–2–2 is not balanced distribution.

(4) *Bid one club.* Only 15 high-card points and no 5-card suit to give you an extra distribution point. (If you missed this one, don't feel badly. The spot cards are strong and many advanced players might open one notrump on this hand. But advanced players can afford to shade their bids, for they play the hands better. One must learn to walk before he can run.)

(5) *Bid one heart.* The distribution is fine for notrump, and you have the right number of points (17 + 1 for the fifth heart), but experience tells us to open the major suit when it is K J x x x or better.

(6) *Bid one club.* You have only 15 high-card points and cannot add a point for the fifth club, since the suit is subpar.

(7) *Bid one notrump.* You have 16 high-card points with satisfactory distribution and stoppers. The only question is whether to open one spade instead. A 10 x x x is not quite respectable enough as a suit so one notrump is the preferred bid.

(8) *Bid one club.* An opening one-notrump bid promises stoppers in *three* suits. Here spades and diamonds are wide open.

Now that we know what a notrump bid is—and what it is not—we can proceed to develop meaningful bidding sequences.

BUILDING ON THE BASE—

RESPONSES

TO ONE NOTRUMP

NOW WE TURN to the other partner, the one who has just heard the good news of an opening one-notrump bid from across the table. (Any time your partner has 16 points, you have reason to rejoice; chances are your team has the balance of strength; if not, it is most unlikely that the opponents have enough for game.)

JUDGING YOUR HAND

Having heard the one-notrump bid, how do you judge your hand? As a matter of fact, you *don't*. You judge the *combined* assets of the partnership and tentatively decide whether to go for part-score, game or slam. For the moment, we will be arbitrary and state that you need a partnership total of 26 points for game. You want to be in game and the only question is whether it is worthwhile to explore for a major-suit fit.

When you have 8 points, partner needs a maximum 18 to give you 26. So it is appropriate to invite game, but you can't insist upon game. Similarly with 9 points, you need 17 from partner; again you suggest game, but this time you can afford to be a bit more bullish about it.

With less than 8 points and no very long suit, there is little hope of game, so you try to find a makable part-score. You pass to one notrump with a balanced hand; with a unbalanced hand, you look for a superior suit contract below game.

GAME WITH 25 POINTS?

There is a logical network of bids to convey these messages and we will deal with them in order. But first, let's see why you need 26 points for game. This is no magic figure, but rather the result of long experience. If you regularly bid game with 25 points combined, you will lose on balance. Superior card players can get away with it, but you shouldn't until you're an expert.

Of course, there *are* 25-point hands that produce game. Here's one:

WEST	EAST
♠ A 7 6	♠ K 8 2
♡ K 8 5 4	♡ 10 9
◇ A 6 2	◇ K 7 4
♣ 8 3 2	♣ A Q J 6 4

East has 14 points (including a distributional point for the fifth club) and West has 11, for a total of 25. South leads a spade against three notrump, and, as it happens, North holds K 7 5 of clubs. Declarer need only enter dummy (West) twice with the ace of spades and ace of diamonds in order to finesse clubs twice, and he has no difficulty in collaring nine tricks—two spades, two diamonds and five clubs.

Now we will switch two cards—the ace and seven of diamonds—and see what happens:

WEST	EAST
♠ A 7 6	♠ K 8 2
♡ K 8 5 4	♡ 10 9
◇ 7 6 2	◇ A K 4
♣ 8 3 2	♣ A Q J 6 4

Still the same 25 points, but divided 18–7. Again South leads a spade and North holds K 7 5 of clubs. But now declarer has only one quick entry to dummy, and unless he is lucky enough to find the ace of hearts with South, he can't get back to dummy to repeat the club finesse. Instead of having an odds-on chance for game (finding K x or K x x of clubs in North's hand), declarer faces odds of about 3 to 1 against him, for he must find *both* a favorable club lie and the ace of hearts onside.

VALUE OF ENTRIES

Entries can be all-important. High cards serve not only as trick winners and stoppers for the opponent's suit, but also as transportation routes to get from one hand to the other. The more evenly the strength is distributed between declarer and dummy, the easier the transport. If your total of 25 points is divided 13 in one hand and 12 in the other, chances are you can get back and forth with ease. We like to be in a game contract with this flexibility, or even if the points are divided 14–11 and possibly 15–10. But after an opening notrump bid, we'll give up the chance for the 25-point game, for the best division we can hope for is 16–9, and it might be 17–8 or even 18–7. This is too top-heavy for our tastes; we won't be able to get to dummy often enough to suit us. The opening notrump, with its guarantee of 16 points, helps to warn us away from these improbable games.

Before leaving this hand, note that in the first example, East is 2 points shy of the point requirement for opening one notrump, and should bid one club. Yet the hand should play in three notrump; competent bidders will get there, for they will recognize the advantage of the even distribution of strength and stretch a point, if necessary, to reach game. With all the emphasis on the opening one-notrump bid, bear in mind that an opening suit bid is also a perfectly acceptable road to a notrump game.

RESPONDER'S POINT VALUATION

After partner opens with one notrump, responder counts points according to the same scale opener uses: ace = 4, king = 3, queen = 2, jack = 1, the fifth and sixth cards in a suit headed by K J or better = 1 distributional point each. But there is one difference: the opener was only concerned with a balanced hand, for that is one of the requirements of an opening notrump bid. The responder's hand may be unbalanced (we say a hand is unbalanced when it contains at least two doubletons, one singleton or one void). An unbalanced hand tends to produce extra tricks at suit play through its ability to shut out high cards in its short suits by ruffing; this buys time to establish small cards in its long suits. Therefore, when you have an unbalanced hand *and are seeking a suit contract,* make the following adjustments:

Add 1 point for each doubleton.
Add 3 points for each singleton.
Add 5 points for each void.

Here's a fair hand to count under this new formula:

♠ None ♡ A Q 7 5 2 ◇ K 9 7 4 ♣ J 7 5 2

There are 10 points in high cards plus 1 for the fifth heart and 5 for the spade void—16 points in all. Together with partner's minimum of 16, that gives you at least 32, or almost in the slam range (usually stated as 33 points). But you really cannot bank on 5 points for the spade void; its true value depends upon partner's spade holding. Take these two hands, for example. With either hand, partner would open one notrump, and we'll assume you land in four hearts:

PARTNER'S HAND

(1) ♠ 6 4 3 ♥ K J 10 9 ♦ Q J 10 ♣ A K Q
(2) ♠ A K Q ♥ K J 10 9 ♦ Q J 10 ♣ 6 4 3

YOUR HAND

♠ None ♥ A Q 7 5 2 ♦ K 9 7 4 ♣ J 7 5 2

Opposite (1), only a very bad break can stop you from taking *twelve* tricks. But with (2), you'll probably be set a trick, as the defense can take three clubs and one diamond.

DUPLICATION OF VALUES

The point count of the two hands is identical. In fact, all we've done is reverse the holding in the black suits. The difference is that in (1) you are getting full value from the 5 points assigned to the spade void, while in (2), this is of practically no value, as your partner's A K Q gives him iron control of the suit. He counts 9 points for his spade holding, while you have counted 5 for your void. That gives a combined total of 14 points in one suit, a clear overassessment of riches. Inevitably one of the other suits will be the "poor cousin" and sure enough, clubs are underfed.

Your *total* point count is but one element in evaluating the playing prospects of your hand; the location of your points is equally important. This holds true even when neither partner is short in the key suit:

PARTNER'S HOLDING   YOUR HOLDING

(1) ♠ x x x   ♠ K x x
(2) ♠ A Q x x x

Opposite (1), you have an expectancy of one-half a trick, assuming that you can get to partner's hand to finesse for the spade ace. Opposite (2), your K x x is worth two tricks to partner, for the combined suit is odds on to produce five tricks.

THE VALUATION CHANGES

Initially you have no choice but to value your K x x as 3 points, for you have to start with some tentative gauge. As the bidding develops, you should increase this valuation if you find the points are working overtime for you, and take away a point or so if they do not fit partner's announced holding in that suit.

Similarly, when an *opponent* bids, you re-evaluate your honors based on your *position*. If your *right-hand opponent* bids a suit, and you hold K J x, it may easily be worth two tricks to you. But the same bid from your *left-hand opponent* deflates your trick expectancy.

CHOICE OF RESPONSE

Now that we have seen some of the pitfalls, and we know that game requires 26 points, let's examine the various bids at our disposal:

1. With 7 points or less—*settle for the best part-score:*
   A. *Pass* with a balanced hand (why increase the level of bidding?).
   B. *Bid two of your best suit*—diamonds, hearts or spades—with an unbalanced hand. Partner is expected to let you play it there. (You cannot play the hand at two clubs, for a two-club bid asks partner to bid again, as we shall see.)
   C. *Bid three in a minor suit* with a 6- or 7-card suit and some hope of making nine tricks. You aim to make a plus score, of course, but your bid also helps to shut the opponents out of the auction.*

2. With 8–9 points and a balanced hand—*bid two notrump* to invite game.
3. With 10 points or more—*make sure of getting to game.*
   A. With a balanced hand of 10–14 points—*bid three notrump* directly.
   B. With a 5-card major—*make a forcing bid of three in your major suit.*
   C. When you know the hand should play at four of your major suit—*bid it directly.*
4. With more than 14 points—*explore for slam.*
   A. Balanced hands—there is a scale of responses to show anywhere from 15 to 21 points, thus enabling partner to place the final contract. This will be covered in Chapter 3.
   B. Unbalanced hands—*bid three of a long major suit* or use the *Stayman Convention.*
5. *The Stayman Convention* starts with a two-club response over a one-notrump opening. It inquires about partner's major-suit holding and is a

---

* This pre-emptive factor dictated a change from the old rule, "The more you bid, the more you have." A few years back, a response of three clubs or three diamonds to an opening notrump was considered a strong bid, but we've found it works out better to rush the bidding when the opponents are marked with strength, and to go slowly when our side has the preponderance of power. Therefore today, the jump to three of a minor is no longer a forcing bid in the Stayman lexicon.

flexible tool for finding the best part-score, game or slam contract. By incorporating this bid into your bidding lexicon, all the other bids outlined above have more precise meanings. Since all the other bids revolve around the Stayman two-club response, we'll examine it first.

THE STAYMAN CONVENTION

A bid of two clubs after partner has opened one notrump and the next hand has passed asks the question, "Do you have a biddable 4-card major suit (Q x x x or better)?" There are three possible rebids from opener:

1. *Two spades,* which says, "I have a biddable 4-card spade suit. If you inquire further, I will tell you about my heart holding."
2. *Two hearts,* which says, "I have a biddable 4-card heart suit, but no biddable 4-card spade suit."
3. *Two diamonds,* which says, "I have neither a 4-card heart nor spade suit headed by a queen or better. Don't take my bid as promising anything about the diamond suit either."*

In effect, opener bids his higher-ranking 4-card major when he has one. Thus, if he bids two hearts, he does not have a 4-card spade suit. But if he bids two spades, he *may* also have a 4-card heart suit. If responder gives him another chance, opener will make it clear whether he indeed has the hearts.

THE WHY OF IT ALL

Why should responder put his partner through all these artificial gyrations? What's the point of it all? Simply to find a superior suit contract. Put another way, responder avails himself of the Stayman Convention when his hand looks as if it will play better in a suit.

WHEN NOT TO USE STAYMAN

A new convention is like an exotic new word just learned. You just can't resist using it, even in inappropriate circumstances. So, at the outset, may we warn you against expecting the Stayman Convention to work miracles on all hands.

---

*Originally, a fourth rebid by opener was permitted—two notrump. This denied holding a biddable 4-card major suit, but affirmed a maximum 18-point hand. The two-diamond rebid gave the same message about the major suits, but showed a 16-to-17-point hand. The two-notrump rebid has since been dropped from the Convention, because it prevented a weak responding hand from using Stayman to find a part-score at the two level.

There are a number of times when you should disdain the Stayman Convention. Among them: when another bid more accurately describes your hand; when you have a balanced hand and no interest in a suit contract; when it is too risky to venture forth; when the exchange of information will help the opponents more than it will your side.

RESPONDER'S REBID

The two-club response is but the first step in the Stayman Convention. To understand its full scope, we must see what responder does with the information of partner's rebid. He now has several courses open to him:

1. He may *pass* opener's rebid if a suit fit has been found and he knows there is no game in the hand.
2. He may *bid a higher-ranking 5-card major suit at the two level.* As long as responder did not pass originally, this promises 8 or 9 points. This rebid—in fact, any rebid by responder—commits the partnership to keep the bidding open until at least two notrump or three of a major suit is reached. If opener has a maximum 18-point notrump, he will see to it that game is reached.*
3. He may rebid *three clubs* or *three diamonds;* this shows length or strength in the suit chosen and at least 10 points. The partnership is thereby committed to game, and proceeds to explore for the best contract. (In the old days, three clubs following two clubs indicated a weak hand, a club bust, and asked partner to pass. But experience has proven that you can get better results by making an immediate three-club bid with such hands, reserving the two club-three club sequence for searching out the best game or slam contract.)
4. If opener has bid responder's 4-card major, responder *raises him*—to the *three level* with 8 or 9– points—to the *four level* with 9+ to 13 points. (When a 4–4 major-suit fit has been found, a good 9 points should give you a fine play for game, even opposite a 16-point notrump hand.)
5. Without a 5-card major suit of his own and with no evidence of a combined 4–4 major-suit fit, responder:
   A. Rebids *two notrump* with 8–9 points, *or*
   B. Rebids *three notrump* with 10–14 points.

---

*Since responder's rebid at the two level "forces" a further bid from opener, this is known as "forcing Stayman"; in the section for advanced partnerships we will encounter a variation known as "non-forcing Stayman," whereby responder's rebid at the two level is usually passed by opener.

EXAMPLES

A few examples will show how smoothly the convention works in practice. In each of the following cases, the bidding has progressed

NORTH	EAST	SOUTH
1NT	Pass	?

and you, South, hold:

(1) ♠ Q 5 2 ♡ Q 6 2 ◇ K 4 3 ♣ 8 6 3 2. *Pass.* There is no reason to look for a better spot or raise the bidding level on balanced hands of 7 points or less. Here the partnership total is 23 points and you expect partner to make the contract.

(2) ♠ 6 5 4 3 ♡ 7 5 3 2 ◇ 6 4 3 ♣ 5 2. *Pass.* The same reasoning applies here, except that your hand is so hopeless that partner hasn't a ghost of a chance to make the contract. That's all the more reason to keep the damage down by staying at the one level. You have gotten past your right-hand opponent; perhaps you will be lucky and your left-hand opponent won't double.

(3) ♠ 6 5 4 3 ♡ 7 5 3 2 ◇ 6 4 3 2 ♣ 5. *Bid two clubs.* Switching the deuce of clubs to the deuce of diamonds makes a world of difference. Now you have an unbalanced hand, and whenever you have a singleton club and four cards in the other three suits, two clubs is the "must" bid. Any 4–4 suit fit at the two level will play better than one notrump, for the opponents won't be able to run the club suit against you. You plan to pass partner's rebid: if it is two hearts or two spades, you are sure of the 4–4 fit. If his rebid is two diamonds, he may have only a 3-card suit, but you may be surprised to know the odds are then 2 to 1 that he has four diamonds.

(4) ♠ 9 7 5 3 ♡ 8 7 4 2 ◇ 9 6 5 3 2 ♣ None. *Bid two clubs.* The case is even stronger with a void in clubs and five diamonds. Now if partner bids two diamonds, it must be the best spot.

(5) ♠ 7 ♡ K 10 5 3 ◇ K J 6 4 ♣ 9 6 5 2. *Pass.* You have an unbalanced hand and would like to bid two clubs, hoping partner will rebid two diamonds or two hearts; you could then pass him in a sound contract. But his most likely call is two spades, because there are so many spades out. Then you'd be stuck; you wouldn't want to pass and any further bid you might make promises 8 points. You can avoid all this trouble by passing at your first turn. Your 7 points should enable partner to make one notrump, so it is losing tactics to experiment and possibly end up with a minus score.

(6) ♠ K 10 5 3 ♡ 7 ◇ K J 6 4 ♣ 9 6 5 2. *Pass.* It is still too risky to bid two clubs. Partner will probably bid two hearts. You could then show your spades at the two level, but would be misrepresenting your hand. (Two spades would show five spades and 8 or 9 points.) Furthermore, two spades would force partner to speak again.

(7) ♠ K 10 5 3 ♡ K J 6 4 ◇ 7 ♣ 9 6 5 2. *Pass.* You have a good chance of finding partner with a 4-card major suit. But if you bid two clubs and he replies two diamonds, you will be in hot water. Why jeopardize the probable plus score you'll get by passing one notrump?

WITH A 5-CARD SUIT

When you have a 5-card or better suit in an unbalanced hand and a part-score is your limit, place the contract directly without recourse to the Stayman Convention. In each of the following cases, the bidding has gone

NORTH	EAST	SOUTH
1NT	Pass	?

and you, South, hold:

(1) ♠ J 7 6 5 4 ♡ 9 6 5 ◇ Q J 4 2 ♣ 6. *Bid two spades.* The hand is worth only 4 points in high cards, but will play much better in a suit. Second choice would be to bid two clubs and pass partner's response. This gives you an excellent chance of finding at least a 4–3 trump fit. The advantage of bidding two spades immediately is you'll probably uncover a 5–3 fit. A pass is out, because partner has small chance of using your small cards in diamonds and spades at a one-notrump contract.

(2) ♠ J 7 6 5 4 ♡ 9 6 5 ◇ Q J 2 ♣ 6 4. *Pass.* The dangerous single-ton has disappeared and this now rates as a balanced hand. There is no reason to think it will play better at two spades than at one notrump.

(3) ♠ 9 8 7 4 3 2 ♡ 5 2 ◇ K 8 6 ♣ 10 9. *Bid two spades.* Always prefer a two-level contract in your 6-card suit to one notrump. At spades, the fourth, fifth and sixth spades will probably win tricks, but what chance does partner have of using them at one notrump?

(4) ♠ K 8 6 ♡ 5 ◇ 10 9 2 ♣ 9 8 7 4 3 2. *Bid three clubs.* Former-ly this was a strong bid in the Stayman System, but now we use it as a pre-emptive bid. There is no way to play the hand at two clubs anyway, since that bid asks partner to name his majors. Therefore you might as well get to your contract quickly so the opponents cannot get into the act.

(5) ♠ K 8 6 ♡ 5 ◇ 9 8 7 4 3 ♣ Q J 10 9. *Bid two diamonds.* There is no necessity to jump when diamonds are your suit. You need a mighty good hand opposite to make three diamonds, so be prudent and play at two diamonds. It is true that the opponents may be able to compete successfully at the two level, but it is foolish to take a minus score deliberately on the chance that they will find their best spot.

(6) ♠ K 8 ♡ 5 ◇ 9 8 7 4 3 2 ♣ 10 9 6 2. *Bid three diamonds.* This hand is stronger in distribution than (5), and you have a better

chance to make three diamonds. Essentially this is a pre-emptive bid: your shortness in the majors should warn you that the opponents are more likely to find a major-suit fit if you give them bidding space at the two level.

(7) ♠ K 10 8 5 2 ♡ K 10 6 2 ◇ 6 3 ♣ 3 2. *Bid two spades.* It is tempting to bid two clubs to allow for partner holding four hearts, so you can pass a two-heart response. But you cannot risk a two-diamond reply. If you then decide to rebid two spades over two diamonds, you misrepresent your hand to partner: this sequence shows 8 points and forces him to speak again.

(8) ♠ K 10 8 5 2 ♡ K 10 6 2 ◇ 6 ♣ Q 3 2. *Bid two clubs.* Now you can afford to bid spades if partner bids two diamonds. Your hand counts to 8 points—just enough for this bidding sequence. If partner obliges you by responding two hearts or two spades, raise his bid.

BIDDING ON GARBAGE

It may have struck you that some of the examples given in this chapter are excessively weak. Hands (2), (3) and (4) on page 31, for example, are complete Yarboroughs.* The odds against holding a hand this bad are about the same as the odds against holding a 30-point hand.

We have deliberately chosen these hands with malice aforethought. It may never have occurred to you to take any action on such garbage—unless a gun were held to your head. It is discouraging enough to pick up a Yarborough, but it reduces the pain somewhat when you can take intelligent action and find a better resting spot. These examples illustrate the mobility of a partnership that lives by disciplined rules with a clear understanding of the meaning of each bid. It would be sheer folly to make any bid on rubbish hands without complete assurance that partner will do what the system tells him to do and let you find the escape spot at the two level.

IMPORTANCE OF PART-SCORES

Deciding where to play the part-score is often taxing. One does not pass out of cowardice, nor does he bid to hear himself speak. The object of either action is to play in the superior part-score contract.

---

*A Yarborough is a hand with no card higher than a nine. The name comes from Lord Yarborough, who reputedly liked to wager with his friends that they would not hold such a hand. He is reputed to have given odds of 1000 to 1, whereas the true odds are 1827 to 1. This makes the good Englishman the only man in history to make money out of Yarboroughs.

Understanding the principles illustrated in the preceding deals will improve your bridge score considerably. There is a vast difference over the year between going down in a part-score contract and carrying it on to the next hand. Matter of fact, two such hands are nearly the equivalent of a game bid and made.

However, it is more exhilarating to bid and make a game on one hand. We'll deal with this phase in the next chapter.

♠ 3 RESPONDER

HAS AMBITIONS

AT LAST we are through with weak responding hands where a part-score is the partnership limit. Now we move on to hands with a point count of 8 or better, which call for a game invitation. The general rule is responder *invites* game with 8–9 points; with more he *insists* upon game.

THE RAISE TO TWO NOTRUMP

Holding a balanced 8- or 9-pointer, responder raises to two notrump. Opener will then pass with a minimum notrump—16 or a bare 17 points—but go on to three notrump with a full 17 or 18.

NORTH	EAST	SOUTH
1NT	Pass	?

You are South and hold:

(1) ♠ A 7 3 ♡ Q 9 ◇ 10 8 3 2 ♣ Q 7 5 3. *Bid two notrump.* Eight scattered points, balanced distribution.

(2) ♠ A K 2 ♡ J 6 5 ◇ 7 6 5 4 ♣ 7 4 2. *Bid two notrump.* Same as (1), except that the strength is concentrated in one suit. But this is no reason to avoid a notrump contract. Opener has already promised stoppers in three suits, so responder doesn't need scattered strength too.

STAYMAN AGAIN

When responder has 8–9 points *and* a 4-card major suit he uses the Stayman two-club response:

(3) ♠ Q 7 5 2 ♡ K 4 2 ◇ K 9 6 3 ♣ 7 5. *Bid two clubs.* Partner will bid two spades if he has four, and you will raise to three, amply showing your 8 points. If he bids two diamonds or two hearts instead, you will rebid two notrump, again revealing your 8 points.

(4) ♠ K 4 2 ♡ Q 7 5 2 ◇ K 9 6 3 ♣ 7 5. *Bid two clubs.* Same reasoning as on (3). But the bidding may develop differently if part-

ner has four cards in both majors. He would then first bid two spades, and you reply two notrump, as before. Opener will then show the hearts if he has them. You will find the major fit if it exists, but it may take longer.

(5) ♠ A 8 3 2 ♡ K 7 5 ◇ Q 9 5 ♣ 8 4 3. *Bid two notrump*. With 4–3–3–3 shape opposite partner's announced balanced distribution, the place to play the hand is at notrump, not at a suit. Use Stayman only when you have *interest* in a major-suit contract, not just because you have 4-card length.

STAYMAN WITH A 5-CARD MAJOR

The auction also proceeds smoothly on hands containing a 5-card major and 8–9 points:

(6) ♠ K 9 6 5 2 ♡ Q 5 2 ◇ 7 ♣ K 9 7 2. *Bid two clubs*. Over two diamonds or two hearts, bid two spades. This logically shows a 5-card suit, because there would be no purpose in showing a four carder when partner's bid denied a 4-card spade suit. (Remember with four spades and four hearts, opener's first response is two spades.) Now partner will raise your spades with any three cards in the suit and will bid notrump with a doubleton. In this way you can explore for a 5–3 suit fit. But you might even find a 5–4 spade fit; if partner bids two spades over two clubs, we recommend a *four*-spade bid with a good partner. His spade bid enhances your hand; it still counts to only 8 high-card points but both the king and the two of spades are more valuable, now that you know partner has four cards in the suit.

(7) ♠ Q 5 2 ♡ K 9 6 5 2 ◇ 7 ♣ K 9 7 2. *Bid two clubs,* again hoping to find a 5–3 or 5–4 fit. This is the same hand as (6), but with the major suits reversed. The difference is that you may miss out on a 5–3 fit if partner bids two spades. Over two spades you can't bid three hearts, for that would overstate your hand and force the partnership into game. Therefore, you have to rebid two notrump. If partner has four hearts, he will show them now. Otherwise, you'll probably land in notrump, despite a possible 5–3 fit. We take special pains to point this out, to demonstrate that no bridge system can cope with every situation. A system is designed to cover the situations that arise most often and present handling problems. In the advanced section of this book, however, we will see how opener with a maximum notrump can give the responder another chance to show a 5-card heart suit. But this luxury requires a supplemental network of bids which is too sophisticated to take up at this time.

FORCE TO GAME WITH 10 POINTS

Responder takes on a more dominant role in the proceedings when he has 10 points or more. No longer need he tender courteous game invitations to his partner, for he is strong enough to insist upon game. With balanced hands of 10–14 points, responder places the final contract directly by an immediate jump to three notrump.

With either of the following hands, responder bids three notrump over partner's one-notrump opening:

    (1)   ♠ K 6 2 ♡ A 5 4 ◇ K J 2 ♣ K 6 5 4

    (2)   ♠ K 9 7 ♡ A 8 ◇ K J 9 3 ♣ K 9 8 4

When responder has some interest in a major-suit contract, he resorts to the versatile Stayman two-club responder. He may hit paydirt the first try:

    (1) ♠ K J 6 5 ♡ A 4 2 ◇ Q 9 4 3 ♣ 6 5. *Bid two clubs.* If partner bids two spades, raise to four. But if partner replies two diamonds or two hearts, you know he doesn't have four spades, so bid three notrump. Note that in either case you bid game at your second turn; it would be a mistake to bid only three spades or two notrump, for these bids would be mere invitations to partner to continue if he has a maximum. With 10 points you want to be in game even if he has a minimum, so you must not give him a chance to let the bidding die short of game.

    (2) ♠ A 4 2 ♡ K J 6 5 ◇ Q 9 4 3 ♣ 6 5. *Bid two clubs,* just as on (1). And again, if partner bids two of your 4-card major, bid game directly in that suit; otherwise jump to three notrump. At first glance you might think you would miss out on a 4–4 heart fit when partner holds both major suits, but this is only an illusion. Partner knows you are interested in the major suits when you bid two clubs. If you don't like spades, you must be looking for hearts, and he will correct the game contract to four hearts holding four cards in that suit.

    (3) ♠ A 6 5 3 ♡ K Q 8 6 ◇ J 5 3 ♣ 9 4. *Bid two clubs.* If partner bids either major, raise his bid to four. Otherwise bid three notrump with confidence that it is the best contract.

Five-card majors are just as easy to handle.

    (4) ♠ K 8 6 5 3 ♡ A K 3 ◇ 6 4 2 ♣ 8 3. *Bid two clubs.* If partner bids two spades, raise him to four. But jump to *three* spades over any other response. This shows five spades and tells partner to bid four spades with any 3-card spade holding, otherwise to bid three notrump. Anytime you jump to three of a major suit, or bid a major suit for the first time at the three level, a game-forcing situation is created.

        An alternative approach is to abandon the Stayman two-club bid and bid three spades on the first round. Again partner is called on to bid four spades with any 3-card (or better) spade holding, and to bid three notrump lacking such a holding. This second approach is more direct and gives away less information to the opponents. If you have a well-developed partnership with a fine player, you might want to work out your own subtle shades of meanings distinguishing between these two sequences. However, in a casual partnership, the two sequences are best played as showing the same kind of hand.

6-CARD SUITS

When Dame Chance has bestowed a 6-card major suit on you, it doesn't take much in the way of points to justify a shot at game. And the best shot is to bid four in your suit right away, and let the opponents struggle to find the right opening lead. The immediate jump to game in your major tells partner you have distributional strength unsuited for notrump play, but offers him no encouragement to make a further bid.

(1) ♠ 10 ♡ K J 10 7 4 2 ◊ K 8 4 ♣ 7 6 4. *Bid four hearts.* The arithmetic is 7 points in high cards, 1 point each for the fifth and sixth hearts and 3 points for the singleton: 12 points in your hand + at least 16 in partner's = a minimum of 28, enough for a very good play for game. You will go down occasionally on this kind of hand when your spade singleton is opposite massed spade strength in partner's hand, leaving gaps in other suits, but in the long run four hearts is the winning bid.

(2) ♠ 8 ♡ K Q J 7 3 ◊ 7 5 ♣ Q J 10 5 3. *Bid four hearts.* Ordinarily this bid shows a 6-card suit, but occasionally you use the bid with a really unbalanced hand and a 5-card major suit. The deciding factor is that your hand is unsuited for notrump, and it is senseless to beat around the bush to find about partner's heart holding. Many players would bid three hearts on this hand on the theory that four hearts is a bad contract unless partner has three cards in the suit. The trouble with this reasoning is partner may hold A x, or 10 x, which is adequate support. In the unlikely event he holds a small doubleton in hearts, chances are you still have a better play for four hearts than three notrump. Partner would probably need a sturdy double stopper in whichever of your two weak suits the opponents attack in order to bring home a notrump game.

GETTING TO SLAM

The road to slam should be a broad, well-lit highway after the helpful opening bid of one notrump. Unfortunately, there are a number of hairpin curves and dangerous intersections when the slam depends upon distributional fit. Many slams are missed because few players know how to look for a suit fit and try for slam after a one-notrump opening. Based on the evidence, this is an advanced phase of the game, so we will defer discussion of it until the second part of the book.

SLAMS ON SHEER POWER

Fortunately, it is ridiculously simple to bid slams that depend on sheer power. We want to be in slam any time our combined assets reach 33 points; the most the opponents can then have is 7 points, or the value of an ace and a king. That means you may be off an ace on top and at worst will need a successful finesse for your slam. Occasionally, you will go down when fate has dealt the opponents the ace and king of the same suit and they cash the first two tricks. But the odds are 15 to 1 against finding this particular holding with the opening leader. If the suit is not opened, you may be able to grab twelve tricks in the other three suits. Besides, there is no regulation that the opponents *must* hold an ace and a king: their 7 points can be made up of scattered queens and jacks. So there are long odds in your favor when you bid 33-point slams.

But it is foolhardy to throw away a near-certain small slam on the flimsy chance for a grand slam. Therefore, keep out of grand slams unless you have at least 37 points in the combined hands. This assures that the other side has at most a king, and at worst, your grand slam will depend upon a finesse.

THE ADDING MACHINE

Getting to these slams is a matter of simple arithmetic. You don't venture forth with 14 points, for even if partner has a maximum 18-pointer, this only gives you 32 in all. But if you have 15 or more, the slam hunt is on.

There is a simple scale of bids that tells your partner precisely how many points you have. He can then add your points to his own and pass short of slam or bid a small slam or grand slam, as the case may be.

Here is the scale:

NUMBER OF POINTS RESPONDER HOLDS	RESPONDER'S BID OVER PARTNER'S 1NT
15	4NT
16	2♣ (Stayman), then 4NT over opener's response
17	5NT
18	2♣, then 5NT
19	6NT
20	2♣, then 6NT
21	7NT

You need *not* memorize this scale. You can re-create it at will when the need arises.

You needn't even memorize the starting point. If you have forgotten it starts at 15 points, just work backward: "I want to be in slam if we have 33 points together; partner's maximum is 18 for his opening one-notrump bid; 33 − 18 = 15, so that is where the scale starts, for there is no reason to plump for slam with less."

All you really need to remember is that the scale progresses 1 point at a time, and obviously the higher you bid, the more points you show. Likewise you show a better hand when you tell your story in two bids, rather than one. Thus two clubs followed by four notrump is stronger than an immediate four notrump.

A COMPLETE SET OF TOOLS

We have seen how responder can invite a game with an 8-to-9-point hand while exploring for a superior major-suit contract. Responder has an expanded kit of bidding tools to find the *right* game contract when holding 10–14 points. Just to recap, he can (1) bid two clubs, Stayman, to find if a 4–4 major-suit fit exists, (2) bid two clubs, Stayman, and later bid his suit to show a 5-card major in hopes of a 5–3 fit, (3) bid three of his long major directly, to find the suit fit, or (4) bid three notrump or four of his 6-card major suit when he can tell from his own hand which is the better contract.

Lastly, with balanced hands of 15 points or more, responder tells partner exactly how many points he has according to an easily derived scale of bids and allows him to place the final contract.

In effect, then, the Stayman Convention enables responder to word his question so precisely that his partner can give a simple direct answer and place the final contract correctly, as we shall see in the next chapter.

④ OPENER DOES

WHAT HE IS TOLD

THE COHESION of the Stayman Convention becomes most apparent when we consider opener's second rebid. Just as with his first response—to two clubs—it is entirely a matter of recognizing the question that he has been asked, and then replying to it.

Holding a minimum notrump—16 or a bare 17 points—he must not take the bidding past two notrump or three of the agreed major; this is the bedrock of "forcing" Stayman.

For a change of pace, we will steer one sample hand through four different sequences:

♠ A Q 3 ♡ K J 7 5 ◊ Q J 3 ♣ K 6 2.

(1)

OPENER	RESPONDER
1NT	2♣
2♡	2NT
?	

Pass. You have shown your one 4-card major and it failed to excite partner. His bidding indicates 8–9 points; you have a minimum 16 for your notrump; thus the total is 24–25, not enough for a good play at game. So now is the time to drop the bidding.

(2)

1NT	2♣
2♡	3♡
?	

Pass. Remember you still have the same minimum and partner still has a maximum of 9 points. Even though a suit fit has been found, you are still short of the combined strength advisable for a game bid.

(3)

1NT	2NT
?	

Pass. Once again, partner has no more than 9 points and there is no likely game in the hand.

(4)

1NT	2♣
2♡	2♠
?	

Bid three spades. You are required to keep the bidding open until two notrump or three of the agreed major is reached. With a supporting holding of three cards in partner's 5-card suit, you must raise. If you had a doubleton spade instead, you would rebid two notrump.

GETTING TO GAME

In the last example (4), responder raises your three-spade bid to four if he has 10 points or more. Similarly, he raises a two-notrump bid to three with such a game-going hand. But more frequently, when responder has enough to insist upon game, he bids it directly at his second turn; then opener need only pass gracefully.

In the following four sequences we will assume that you are the opener and have the same 16-point hand given earlier:

♠ A Q 3   ♡ K J 7 5   ◊ Q J 3   ♣ K 6 2.

	OPENER	RESPONDER	
(1)	1NT	2♣	*Pass.* Partner has already put the partnership
	2♡	4♡	in game and shown no interest in slam. It is
	?		your duty to pass like a gentleman (or lady).
(2)	1NT	2♣	*Pass.* Partner doesn't like hearts and has no 5-
	2♡	3NT	card spade suit—see (4), page 37—so three
	?		notrump must be the best game contract.
(3)	1NT	3NT	*Pass.* Partner has no interest in the majors, so
	?		there is no reason to disturb the contract.

It is even simpler when partner bids game at his first turn:

	OPENER	RESPONDER	
(4)	1NT	4♡ or 4♠	*Pass.* Sure, you have fine support for partner's
	?		suit. But his bid shows no slam interest. Remember, after you open one notrump, partner is the captain of the team—the one who asks the questions. He hasn't asked any here, so don't offer any answers.

When your major suit is spades, one more sequence is possible. To illustrate, we will reverse the major-suit holdings of the given hand:

♠ K J 7 5   ♡ A Q 3   ◊ Q J 3   ♣ K 6 2.

OPENER	RESPONDER	
1NT	2♣	*Bid four hearts.* When responder names a major
2♠	3♡	suit at the three level for the first time, a game-
?		forcing situation is created. Here he is showing a 5-card heart suit and you should be delighted to raise with A Q x (in fact, you should raise with any three or more cards in hearts).

For the moment, we will defer discussion of opener's action when he holds both major suits.

WHEN OPENER HAS BETTER THAN A MINIMUM

If you have a good 17 points or more as opener and partner has indicated 8–9 points, it is up to you to make sure the partnership gets to game:

♠ A Q 3 ♡ K J 7 5 ◊ Q J 3 2 ♣ A J.

	OPENER	RESPONDER	
(1)	1NT	2♣	*Bid four hearts.* The suit fit has been found and you have a maximum 18-pointer. Note that your two-heart bid did not indicate whether you were maximum or minimum.
	2♡	3♡	
	?		
(2)	1NT	2♣	*Bid three notrump.* There is no major-suit fit, but you hold 26 points between the two hands.
	2♡	2NT	
	?		
(3)	1NT	2NT	*Bid three notrump.* Partner has 8–9 points, and you have a maximum, so there should be a good play for game.
	?		
(4)	1NT	2♣	*Bid four spades.* When you want to be in game, don't leave it up to partner. You have found a good 5–3 spade fit, so bid the game in spades. If you had a doubleton spade, your proper rebid would be three notrump.
	2♡	2♠	
	?		

WITH BOTH MAJORS

When opener has both major suits, two additional sequences are possible:

	OPENER	RESPONDER
(1)	1NT	2♣
	2♠	2NT
	?	
(2)	1NT	2♣
	2♠	3NT
	?	

Responder would have raised in spades with 4-card support. He would not have used Stayman without four cards in one of the majors. Therefore, he must have four hearts.

Opener has a clear duty to correct to the superior contract. In sequence (1), he bids four hearts; in sequence (2), he bids four hearts with better than a minimum, otherwise three hearts.

A MINOR AT THE THREE LEVEL

The most subtle sequences stem from responder's rebid of three clubs or three diamonds following his two-club query. Should you raise the suit? What do you need in the suit to raise? Does a raise show a maximum notrump? And behind all these questions is the nagging reluctance to go past the three-notrump level.

This is not a new dilemma, but the same old devil in new cloth. If you have used Stayman for some time, you encountered the same problem when partner responded three clubs or three diamonds to your opening notrump. Until recent years, the direct response of three in a minor showed a strong hand and interest in the minor suit bid, and created a game-forcing situation.

Today, of course, opener has no problem after an immediate three-club or three-diamond response, for those bids have been redefined as weak pre-emptive bids and opener can pass gratefully.

But the sequence that has taken its place—two clubs followed by three clubs (or three diamonds)—brings us back to the same bugaboo. The responder's message is, "I have enough strength to force to game, plus length in the minor suit I bid. Tell me more about your hand."

This sequence introduces new shades of meaning and subtler development of the auction. Each sequence has its own logical meaning, but the inferences are delicate and full discussion of this properly belongs in the second part of the book, the section for advanced players.

In a casual bridge game or with an unfamiliar partner, the opening bidder:

1. Bids three notrump if he has no better message to deliver. This bid reaffirms a moderate notrump and advises that all unbid suits are stopped.

2. Bids a new suit at the three level when he lacks a stopper in a side suit. In effect, opener thereby informs his partner that there is a flaw in his hand for notrump. By inference, the bid of a new suit also confirms a fit with partner's suit, for opener could not have bid notrump with *two* suits unstopped.

Opener chooses the side suit in which he has the most concentrated strength. Thus, in the sequence:

OPENER	RESPONDER
1NT	2♣
2♦	3♣
3♠	

opener's last bid indicates his spade holding has the most concentrated strength of the three unbid suits (we don't count diamonds as a bid suit, since this response was artificial). Note that the opener shows his *strength*, not his length; his previous two-diamond bid denied a 4-card spade holding.

There is no reason to raise the minor suit immediately and waste a round of bidding. Far better to use the three level to tell partner where opener has massed strength, for this will help him decide whether to go on to a minor-suit game or slam or settle for three notrump.

This approach has a dual purpose: it permits useful exchange of information and is unlikely to land you in the wrong spot with a partner unfamiliar with these responses.

IF PARTNER MISUNDERSTANDS

Isn't this approach dangerous with a partner who has never heard of these nuances? Not really. If the auction has progressed:

SOUTH	NORTH
1NT	2♣
2◇	3◇
3♡	?

North may be puzzled, but at least he knows you have something in hearts. If he needs help in hearts, he will be encouraged and perhaps push on to a makable slam. If he has a singleton heart, he may properly evaluate the duplication of values and, reassured about his weak suit, settle for three notrump.

The worst that can happen is that he raises your heart "suit" to four. But you can correct to five diamonds. Perhaps he will then realize that you (1) liked diamonds all along and (2) have top-card strength, not length, in hearts.

Another possibility is that when he hears your three-heart bid, he will be so confused that he will rebid three notrump for lack of anything better. And, who knows, three notrump may even be a better contract. If you can't explore a minor-suit slam intelligently with your partner-of-the-moment, you might as well contract for a nine-trick game at notrump, rather than eleven tricks at a minor.

It is much more reassuring to play with a reliable partner who won't misconstrue your bids. When you find such a partner and have mastered the essential elements of notrump bidding and the Stayman Convention, you are ready for Part II, which outlines the manifold uses of the "double minor" response in Chapter 10.

⟨5⟩ THE OPPONENTS SPEAK UP

EXPERIENCED PLAYERS overcall at the one level quite freely, for they know how tough it is to make a penalty double pay off at this range. To catch the culprit at all and inflict a double, one of his opponents must have trump length but the other opponent usually runs from the double because he is short in the suit; or the overcaller's partner takes out into his own suit. Even when the double of a one-bid is left in, it rarely shows a profit. A two- or three-trick set is no grand accomplishment if you had a biddable game your way. For these reasons most seasoned players don't even bother to double for penalties at the one level except in extraordinary circumstances.

But the *two* level is another kettle of fish. The opener's partner has been deprived of the smooth flow of the auction and will settle for a juicy penalty one level higher instead of a shot at a problematical game.

It is particularly risky to overcall a strong opening one-notrump bid, for the opener has announced that he has at least 40 percent of the deck's high-card strength. His partner needs only a few scattered high cards to inflict a devastating penalty double of a reckless overcall.

Still, there are times when an adventuresome opponent takes the bit in his mouth. And yes, you will also encounter overcalls which are eminently sound. Thus, as responder you cannot double automatically with a few points; yet you must be on your toes to collect your full toll when an adversary steps out of line.

Make no mistake about the nuisance value of the overcall. It disturbs the smooth flow of the auction, gives the overcaller's partner an opportunity to outbid you or sacrifice, perhaps indicates the killing opening lead if your side buys the contract. These are very real disadvantages for your team, so you must take effective countermeasures.

WHEN TO DOUBLE FOR PENALTIES

It would be comforting to be able to wait until you are sitting over the over-caller with something like K J 9 8 in his suit and a couple of points outside. This, of course, is the ideal double, for it looks as if you have three trump tricks the opponents didn't figure on losing. If you have 6 points, your partner has 16, and the overcaller has, say 14, for his bid, there are only some 4 points left for the overcaller's partner. The rash intruder will have to play out of his own hand most of the way and he is in for a rocky time. To cap it all off, your side lacks the strength for a game of your own, so a juicy penalty is that much more welcome.

As a practical matter, you will seldom hold anything like K J 9 8 in the op-ponent's suit, and if you wait for this surefire double, you'll let the opponents off the hook far too often. We recommend that you double on any balanced hand of 7 points that includes three cards in the opponent's suit; 6 points in high cards will suffice with four trumps. Most of the time you'll show a hand-some profit; occasionally the contract will be made, but it is a hoary bridge axiom that if the opponents never make a doubled contract against you, you are not doubling often enough.

The more unbalanced your hand, the dimmer the prospects for a double. The overcaller is probably short in your long suit and will ruff away the tricks you were counting on. It is better to go after your own contract, whether part-score or game. But use the information the overcall has given you. Figure him for some high-card points, a fairly good and long suit, and shortness in one or two suits.

If you have to finesse toward partner's hand, the odds are that the overcaller will have most of the missing high cards. Likewise, since the overcaller is short in some suit, it could easily be the one you choose as trump; don't be too op-timistic about a favorable trump break. Use all this evidence in choosing your action. Then if you decide to bid a touchy game, don't pretend to be sur-prised if the overcaller's partner doubles. All he needs is some trump length and a side winner or so, for he can count on his partner's bid for one or two defensive tricks.

HOW TO COMPETE

First of all, there is no mandate that you must compete. A worthless hand still calls for a pass, overcall or no overcall; the intervening bid has not im-proved it. But sometimes the overcall may influence you to bid on a hand that you would otherwise pass. You might have been very happy to settle for a one-notrump part-score for your side, but now that an opponent has intervened, you don't want to let him buy the contract dirt cheap. If you have the where-

withal, it is wise to compete. If you go down a trick or two and deprive the opponents of their part-score, it is probably a good investment. Perhaps they
will take the push and get up a trick too high and you will end up with a plus
score on a hand that "belonged" to them.

AT THE TWO LEVEL

Following an overcall of opener's notrump, a bid of two in a suit is limited
and competitive (just as if there had been no overcall). Likewise, if the opening
notrumper raises the bid to the three level, it is also competitive and it is a
breach of partnership faith for responder to raise to four. If the opener has
visions of game, he will bid a new suit instead of raising.

	SOUTH	WEST	NORTH	EAST
(1)	1NT	2♢	2♡	Pass
	3♡			
(2)	1NT	2♢	2♠	3♢
	3♠			
(3)	1NT	2♢	2♠	Pass
	3♣ (or 3♡)			
(4)	1NT	2♢	2♠	Pass
	3♢			

In (1) and (2), South's raise is purely competitive. In the first case, no new competition has arisen since the overcall, but the bid is insurance that West won't
be able to show a second suit cheaply. South should have a 4-card or better
trump holding for this pre-emptive action. In (2), the need to compete is very
real, since East has raised the overcall.

Sequence (3) shows game interest on South's part which can only be based
on a maximum notrump and a spade fit. If North has good values for his bid,
he now bids four spades; if not, he merely returns to three spades. In choosing
between hearts and clubs for his invitation, South will presumably bid the suit
in which he has better top-card strength.

On the same theory, (4) indicates diamond strength. South's full message
is the essence of logic: "I still have hope for game, for I have a maximum notrump and a fine fit in your suit. I also have a very good stopper in diamonds
and I'm suggesting a notrump contract as a possible alternative to four
spades."

Most of the time, however, the opening notrumper will pass over his partner's two-level response. Sequence (1), for example, is comparatively rare

and South would have to have some reason for feeling further competition is in the air before jeopardizing a probable plus score by going one trick higher

Sequences (3) or (4) are equally unlikely, for South needs both a maximum notrump *and* a spade fit. But our bidding system has to allow for all these possibilities.

AT THE THREE LEVEL

A response of three in a *minor* suit is competitive and the opener is expected to pass. But there are exceptions:

SOUTH	WEST	NORTH	EAST
1NT	2♠	3♣	Pass
?			

South holds:

(1) ♠ A Q 7 ♡ J 10 4 2 ◇ K J 4 ♣ A K 2. *Bid three notrump.* You have a maximum notrump, a fine fit in clubs and the opponent's suit securely stopped, so there is a fine prospect for game. But note you need all three.

SOUTH	WEST	NORTH	EAST
1NT	2♠	3◇	3♠
?			

South holds:

(1) ♠ 6 5 4 3 ♡ A 5 ◇ K Q 5 ♣ A K 4 2. *Bid four diamonds* as a competitive move. You should size up the situation thusly: "My partner probably has, at most, a singleton spade; none of my strength is in spades, so we have no wasted values there. Similarly, one of the opponents may have a singleton club, or singleton diamond. They will probably make three spades, and we might easily make four diamonds, or go down a trick to save the part-score. So, with this particular minimum notrump, I choose to compete."

Judging these competitive situations is one of the most difficult areas of bridge, and only general advice can be given. In the long run, you will do better to play the hand when you have a strong combined trump suit; don't compete too strenuously with broken trump holdings, for you may take a substantial loss aiming at a small profit whenever you hit a bad trump break.

"WAS I RIGHT?"

Whatever your decision on a specific hand, you will not know if it was "correct" until all four hands are spread on the table. Since you cannot know the exact composition of each hand during the bidding, perhaps there is no "correct" solution. Even the post-mortem may not reveal the truth. Unsuccessful declarers are very prone to reassuring statements like "It was a good sacrifice; they could have made their vulnerable game; both finesses are on side." Maybe. But if he were allowed to play the hand, the opposing declarer would perhaps take what is charmingly known as a "different view." Or a keen defensive play or deceptive maneuver might have led him astray. And just possibly, he might have misplayed the hand all by himself. Nobody will ever know, since he never had the chance to prove his mettle on that particular hand.

If you look to the quality of your trump suit you will avoid the disastrous penalties. Confidentially, you don't have to be a brilliant player to win at bridge; as long as the others make more mistakes than you do, you will continue collecting their money. Remember the legend that in the land of the blind, the one-eyed man is king?

Yet your partner can throw you for a bundle at any given moment. *That's* the man you have to worry about—not the opponents. It is not the purpose of this book to tell you how to live with the odd characters who turn up as your partners from time to time. But we can pass along one bit of advice: it doesn't pay to holler, lecture or scream at them. Each of them thinks he is a fine bridge player who ran into a horrible bit of luck—and he'll do it to you again the next time.

Every once in a while, though, you need to let off some steam. There is a limit to how much partnership punishment anyone can take; one of the joys of playing bridge is that you can holler at your partner without worrying whether it will set off World War III or send the stock market tumbling.

Let's return to your cheerful partner who "saved" a vulnerable game. Say, it *only* cost you 500 points. When he is through crowing, point out to him that the odds of winning two out of two finesses are only 1 in 4, so the enemy's expectation in the long run is not 600 points, but only one-fourth of that, or 150 points. Ask him why then he regards a price of more than three times that figure as such a bargain. He will probably glare and repeat, "They would have made it, wouldn't they?" Your answer should be a soft "We'll never know! Whose deal is it?" To repeat, you never win these arguments, but at least you don't have to get terribly wrought up over this one, for you have the facts on your side.

MAJOR SUITS AT THE THREE LEVEL

Back to the business at hand: a free bid in a *major* suit at the three level is forcing to game. Opener raises to four with any three cards in partner's suit. Otherwise he bids three notrump.

NORTH	EAST	SOUTH	WEST
1NT	2♠	3♡	Pass
?			

You, North, hold:

(1) ♠ A 5 2 ♡ K J ◇ A Q 8 5 ♣ K 6 4 3. *Bid four hearts* in preference to the "book" bid of three notrump. Unless partner produces a second spade stopper, you may have no play at all for
three notrump. But there should be a much better play at four
hearts even with a 5–2 trump suit. No guarantees go with the bid,
though; West could have four (or five!) hearts and punish you with
with a double. Bridge is not always an easy game.

It is usually comforting to hear partner jump the bidding, but here is one
case where a jump doesn't change the meaning of the bid. As long as partner
bids his major suit at the three level, it means the same thing:

	SOUTH	WEST	NORTH
(1)	1NT	2♡	3♠
(2)	1NT	2♠	3♡

In both cases North is showing the same amount of strength and is making
a game force.

In all the examples thus far, the enemy has overcalled at the two level.
However, the same considerations apply if the opponent makes a jump overcall at the three level. Partner's overcall in a major suit is forcing to game, but
a three-diamond bid over a three-club overcall is purely competitive.

There is a shade of difference in deciding whether to double at the three
level. When responder has enough strength for game, he may choose a penalty double instead of bidding game; doubling offers greater rewards at the
three level than at the two level. Which course he chooses is a matter of his
holding and his taste; frequently the deciding factor is the length and strength
in the opponent's suit.

CUE-BIDS

The pesky overcall has gotten you past the two-club level, so the Stayman
two-club response is no longer available. An immediate cue-bid in the opponent's suit solves the problem nicely. It is best played as a force to game:
there simply isn't enough bidding room to invite a game *and* look for a
4–4 major-suit fit.

	SOUTH	WEST	NORTH
	1NT	2◇	?

North holds:

(1)   ♠ A 10 6 5 ♡ K J 7 5 ◇ 6 ♣ Q 5 3 2. *Bid three diamonds.* Whichever major partner bids you will raise to four. If he bids three notrump instead, pass and hope he can stop the diamond suit.

AFTER A DOUBLE

Most of the time a double of your partner's opening notrump means nothing but trouble. If you had planned to bid your suit at the two level, by all means make the same bid after the double; your trump length will act to prevent any real disaster. If you have a balanced hand and no run-out suit, you have to decide whether to sit tight and hope for the best or whether to try to find a 4-3 (or hopefully, a 4-4) suit that will play better at the two level. (See S.O.S. Redouble, p. 156.)

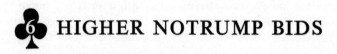

HIGHER NOTRUMP BIDS

THE UPPER LIMIT ot an opening one-notrump bid is 18 points. But when your cards are running well, you may pick up balanced hands of greater strength. You will then want to define your hand to partner and explore for the optimum contract. This chapter explains how to handle such hands and how the subsequent bidding develops.

HANDS OF MORE THAN 18 POINTS

A scale has been worked out for notrump-type hands counting to more than 18 points:

NUMBER OF POINTS OPENER HOLDS	OPENER'S BID
18+, 19 or 20–	1 of a suit, jump to 2NT on the next round; if partner's response comes at the two level, jump to 3NT
20+ or 21–	1 of a suit, jump to 3NT on the next round
21+ to 24–	2NT
24+ to 27	3NT

The +'s and −'s on this scale indicate that there is some overlap and that is where judgment comes in. You should think more highly of your hand—and give it a plus value—when it contains good intermediaries like tens and nines, when the queens and jacks are in combination with other honors rather than alone, or when the hand is rich in aces and kings. Without these features, devalue the hand and give it a mental minus.

WITH WEAK TWO-BIDS

Many players today use the opening bids of two diamonds, two hearts and two spades as pre-emptive bids, reserving two clubs as the only force to game. These players have the opportunity of introducing two new sequences into the above scale: an opening two-club bid followed by a minimum rebid in no-trump and an opening two-club bid followed by a jump in notrump. This enables them to define each bid on the notrump scale with a narrower range. If you use weak two-bids, or play against people who do, refer to page 173, which explains the revised scale. For the moment, it is sufficient to note that two clubs followed by a notrump bid shows a stronger hand than an immediate notrump bid of the same denomination, e.g., two clubs-two notrump shows a better hand than a two-notrump opening bid.

STRONGER HANDS

Our scale stops at 27 points. It is possible to construct a scale for stronger hands, but they occur so infrequently that it is hardly worthwhile to memorize the requirements. Besides, your partner-of-the moment might not be as knowledgeable as you and get you to some impossible contract. Our advice is to open hands of 28 points or more with a game-forcing bid and decide your subsequent actions as the bidding develops.

THE DELAYED JUMP IN NOTRUMP

Opening bids of two notrump and three notrump guarantee stoppers in all four suits. In one sense, a *jump* in notrump following a suit opening conveys the same message. However, in this case all the stoppers need not be in your own hand; you may assume partner has the necessary stopper in the suit he bid.

Sometimes you know exactly what you will rebid when you open in a suit:

(1) ♠ Q J 10 ♡ A Q ◇ K Q J 10 6 ♣ K J 10. *Bid one diamond.* Rebid two notrump over any nonjump suit response. If partner responds one notrump, jump to three notrump.

More often, though, your second bid depends upon partner's response:

(2) ♠ J 6 2 ♡ A Q J 6 3 ◇ A K 7 ♣ K 5. *Bid one heart.* If partner bids one spade, jump to two notrump, for you know all four
suits are stopped. Over a one-notrump response, jump to three notrump, counting on him to help stop the spades. But after a two-
club or two-diamond response, you cannot jump in notrump for
lack of spade stopper, so you must choose the most descriptive
suit rebid. Over a raise to two hearts, bid either three or four
hearts, as the spirit moves you.

(3) ♠ A J 6 ♡ 8 5 2 ◇ A K 6 ♣ A Q J 7. *Bid one club.* You hope
partner will respond one heart, so you can jump to two notrump.
If he responds one notrump, take a shot at three of the same. But
after a diamond or spade response, you have a problem. Without
a heart stopper you cannot bid notrump, and your choice of suit
response will depend upon your mood of the moment, your partner of the moment, the lateness of the hour and perhaps sundry
other factors.

Let's dispense with two troublesome matters before we proceed further:

1. WHEN THREE CLUBS IS NOT STAYMAN

After your side opens the bidding with one of a suit and later bids notrump,
a further bid in clubs is *not* Stayman. The theory is that you have already ex-
changed information about your suit holdings, and a club bid has its natural
meaning.

	NORTH	SOUTH
(1)	1♡	1♠
	2NT	3♣
(2)	1♠	2♡
	2NT	3♣
(3)	1♣	1◇
	2NT	3♣

In (1) and (2) South is showing a club suit. In (3) he is supporting partner's
club suit.

2. SIGN-OFF BY RESPONDER

What does South's bid mean in the following sequence:

	NORTH	SOUTH
	1◇	1♡
	2NT	3♡

Many players interpret three hearts as a forward-going bid, but that must be incorrect. If South has a game-going hand and a 6-card suit, he can bid four hearts himself. If he has a 5-card suit in a game-going hand, he can bid three clubs or three diamonds to give North the chance to show delayed heart support with a tripleton. And, of course, if South wants to be in three no-trump, nothing prevents him from saying the magic words. Add it all up and it is a bit naive for North to think his partner is looking for game.

By elimination, then, we see that South is trying to sign off at three hearts. Apparently he just scratched up a response to one diamond on the basis of a long heart suit. He may have a hand like

♠ 9 8 4 ♡ K J 10 9 8 4 ◇ 6 ♣ 8 6 2.

If North insists on rebidding three notrump with something like

♠ A 7 5 ♡ Q 5 ◇ A Q J 2 ♣ K Q 6 4

he will be lucky to make six tricks.

Review the bidding and notice that South judged the situation nicely each step of the way. He rightly refused to pass one diamond, an inferior contract that will probably go down. He took his partner out of a losing two notrump spot. He wants to play at three hearts, which should make comfortably; and he's quite right to drop the bidding at a part-score, for there is a poor play for four hearts. After South has proved to be such a helpful partner and a bright fellow, it is criminal for North to hang him out of ignorance.

But North is not barred from the auction by any means. If he has a good fit in partner's suit and sees a chance to run nine tricks, he should bid three notrump. Here is just such a hand:

♠ A 7 5 ♡ A Q 3 ◇ A Q 7 5 ♣ K 9 4.

A club or diamond lead hands declarer his ninth trick immediately; with any other lead, he can make the hand on a successful finesse. Incidentally, four hearts is an inferior contract, for it may require winning finesses in both minor suits and the odds are almost 3 to 1 against.

FORWARD ACTION BY RESPONDER

By way of contrast responder's bid in a *new* suit—or his delayed raise of opener's suit—following opener's jump to two notrump creates a game-forcing situation.

NORTH	SOUTH		NORTH	SOUTH
1◇	1♡		1◇	1♡
2NT	3♣		2NT	3◇

North must keep the bidding open in both these sequences.

THE OPENING BID OF TWO NOTRUMP

This bid gives a very specific message. It promises:

1. A point count of 21+ to 24− points.
2. Balanced distribution: 4-3-3-3, 4-4-3-2 or 5-3-3-2 (the last only if the 5-card suit is a minor).
3. Stoppers in all four suits.

Test yourself on these hands:

(1) ♠ A J 3 ♡ K 6 4 ◇ A K Q J 2 ♣ K 4. *Bid two notrump.* You have 21 points plus an extra point for the fifth diamond. The shape is balanced and all suits are stopped.

(2) ♠ A J 3 ♡ A K Q J 2 ◇ K 6 4 ♣ K 4. *Bid one heart.* When your 5-card suit is a major, it is more prudent to open one in a suit.

(3) ♠ A Q 10 ♡ A K Q ◇ 7 5 3 ♣ A K J 4. *Bid one club.* You have no stopper in diamonds, and a two-notrump opening demands stoppers in all four suits.

RESPONSES TO TWO NOTRUMP

After a two-notrump opening, any bid by responder commits the partnership to reach game. Here, in a nutshell, is the meaning of each response:

1. *Pass:* Usually less than 5 points. Responder has given up hope for game.

2. *Three diamonds, three hearts or three spades:* Responder shows a 5-card suit and a willingness to go to game; the bid is forcing, but does not necessarily show a strong hand. The opener is asked to raise the suit with support or rebid three notrump without good support; responder usually passes opener's rebid.

3. *Four hearts or four spades:* A 6-card suit in an unbalanced hand unsuited for notrump. Not a strong hand; opener is expected to pass unless he has a maximum, mostly in aces and kings, and a fine fit for the suit.

4. *Three notrump:* 5-10 points. Responder's hand is sufficiently balanced to play at notrump and not sufficiently strong to suggest slam.

5. *Three clubs:* The Stayman Convention, inquiring about major suits. Opener's rebids are the same as for one notrump, but one level higher.

EXAMPLES

The distinctions between bids will become clear as we examine sample hands. In each case the bidding has proceeded:

NORTH	WEST	SOUTH
2NT	Pass	?

and you, South, hold:

(1) ♠ Q 4 3 ♡ 6 5 4 2 ◇ 8 6 4 2 ♣ Q 6. *Pass*. With less than 5 points and a balanced hand, game is unlikely.

(2) ♠ J 8 7 6 3 ♡ 10 5 2 ◇ 8 7 4 ♣ Q 6. *Pass*. You would like to play in three spades but any bid over two notrump is forcing to game.

(3) ♠ 8 4 ♡ K J 9 6 5 ◇ 7 5 4 ♣ J 8 3. *Bid three hearts*. You have enough for game, but should give the opener his choice whether to play at three notrump or four hearts. If opener holds ♠ K Q 7 ♡ A Q 8 3 ◇ A 10 ♣ A Q 5 4, for example, he will raise your three-heart bid to four hearts. This is a far superior contract to three notrump.

(4) ♠ K J 10 7 6 5 ♡ 8 ◇ Q 7 6 4 ♣ 5 2. *Bid four spades*. You want to be in game but there is no hope for slam; you know where the hand should play, so there is no point in giving partner a choice.

(5) ♠ 6 5 ♡ J 10 7 6 5 4 3 ◇ 6 4 ♣ 5 2. *Bid four hearts*. This may look like a lot of bidding on very little, but the picture improves when you place it next to a typical opening two-notrump bid: ♠ A K 7 ♡ A 2 ◇ A J 5 2 ♣ K Q 8 3. This is a minimum two-notrump hand and the heart support is less than exciting. Nonetheless, the four-heart contract makes if the outstanding trumps are divided 2–2 or either opponent holds a singleton honor. The odds are about 5 to 3 in your favor.

(6) ♠ Q 9 5 ♡ K 6 4 ◇ 9 8 4 ♣ 10 9 7 6. *Bid three notrump*. Five points and no interest in the major suits.

(7) ♠ K 7 3 ♡ J 5 ◇ K J 6 2 ♣ 9 7 3 2. *Bid three notrump*. It is possible there is a slam, if partner holds a maximum notrump, bristling with aces and kings and a good fit in diamonds. But there is no way to explore at a safe level.

(8) ♠ 10 8 6 3 ♡ K 8 7 4 ◇ 7 2 ♣ Q 5 3. *Bid three clubs*. This is, of course, Stayman, and you plan to raise a major-suit response to four. If partner bids three diamonds, you can bid three notrump, knowing you've explored the major-suit route and have enough points to contribute toward the notrump game.

(9) ♠ Q 8 7 2 ♡ Q 9 5 4 ◇ 6 2 ♣ 7 6 5. *Pass*. You would like to explore a major-suit game via Stayman, but if partner lacks a 4-card major, he is not going to like your hand as dummy in a three-notrump contract. You are a point shy for a notrump raise.

(10) ♠ A J 6 4 ♡ 9 7 3 ◇ 8 6 ♣ 7 5 3 2. *Bid three clubs*. It is usually worthwhile to look for the major-suit fit when you have only one 4-card major to offer. The exception occurs when you have a 4–3–3–3 hand.

(11) ♠ J 8 7 6 5 ♡ A 2 ◇ 9 7 3 ♣ 8 4 2. *Bid three spades*. This allows partner to choose between a four-spade and three-notrump contract. An alternate approach is to bid three clubs, Stayman,

and rebid three spades over a red-suit response. This again shows five spades and offers partner the final option on placing the contract. There is little to choose between the two approaches; three clubs followed by three spades *sounds* just a mite stronger.

(12) ♠ 10 8 4 ♡ 9 ◇ 10 9 8 7 4 ♣ K 8 7. *Bid three diamonds.* You have enough to bid three notrump immediately, but if partner is weak in hearts, your singleton won't cheer him any. It costs nothing to show partner your diamonds. Partner might have: ♠ A K J ♡ Q 8 3 ◇ A J 6 3 ♣ A Q J. He'd squirm in three notrump, but needs only a successful finesse to make five diamonds.

(13) ♠ K 10 8 5 4 ♡ 10 9 6 3 2 ◇ 7 5 ♣ 4. *Bid three spades.* If partner rebids three notrump, bid four hearts, giving him his choice of the two majors. While you have only 3 high-card points, you have great distributional strength. Since you know the hand will play in one of your suits, you can count 1 point for the doubleton and 3 for the singleton. That raises your total to a respectable 7 points, plenty for game.

OPENER'S REBID

After opening with two notrump and hearing partner's response, opener's action is fairly cut-and-dried.

After a three-club Stayman response: Opener rebids in the same fashion as when he has opened one notrump and been confronted with a Stayman inquiry. He bids three spades if he holds Q x x x or better in spades, three hearts if he lacks a biddable spade suit but has a heart holding as good as Q x x x—and three diamonds without any biddable major suit. If responder now rebids a suit at the three level, showing a five carder, opener raises to four with any reasonable 3-card support, particularly when he has a sketchy stopper like Q x x in a side suit.

After this sequence:

OPENER	RESPONDER
2NT	3♣
3♠	3NT

opener should bid four hearts with a biddable 4-card heart suit. Responder wouldn't have used Stayman if he did not have four cards in one of the majors. Since it did not prove to be spades, it must be hearts, and four hearts figures to be a safer contract.

After a three-spade, three-heart or three-diamond response: Opener rebids three notrump or raises partner's suit to four. If the response was three of a major suit, opener generally raises to four with any reasonable 3-card support in the suit, particularly when he has a minimum stopper in one of the side suits. Lacking such 3-card support, opener rebids three notrump. The responder may still place the final contract at four of his major, but at least opener has had the chance to express his preference.

Replying to three diamonds is another matter. If all the side suits are adequately protected, opener may choose to rebid three notrump even with good diamond support. In general, it will be easier to make nine tricks at notrump than eleven at diamonds. But with a loosely guarded side suit, opener will raise diamonds and go for the safer game.

BIDDING SLAM ON SHEER POWER

A notrump raise past the game level is the time-honored way to get to slam after an opening two-notrump bid. These raises are based on balanced hands with 10 points or more according to the following scale:

NUMBER OF POINTS RESPONDER HOLDS	RESPONDER'S BID OVER PARTNER'S 2NT
10	4NT
11	3♣ (Stayman), then 4NT over opener's response
12	5NT
13	3♣, then 5NT
14	6NT
15	3♣, then 6NT
16 and over	7NT

Don't bother to commit this table to memory. Just remember the starting point and you can work out the proper response when the occasion arises at the table. Opener's maximum count for his two-notrump bid is 24— points, so you need 10 points to suggest slam, and that is where the table starts. Also note that a two-step response shows one point more than the immediate bid at the same level. Thus, three clubs-five notrump is a point better than the immediate response of five notrump.

Opener adds the points shown by the response to his own to determine the final contract. A small slam should be bid when the partnership holds 33 points, and a grand slam when they total 37 points.

INTERFERENCE

It is rare that an opponent ventures an overcall after an opening two-notrump bid, but in the game of bridge you must be prepared for all eventualities. Responder must be on the alert to double for penalties. If the double has no appeal, he ignores the overcall and makes the same bid he would have made without the interference. Thus a raise to three notrump may be made without a stopper in the opponent's suit.

OPENING THREE-NOTRUMP BIDS

Once in a blue moon you will hold a balanced hand of 24 points or more. Even experts tend to get bullish with such goodies. In the flush of excitement it is so easy to plunge into game without stopping to figure what you need from partner to make it a good gamble.

Say that you hold this hand:

♠ K Q 3 ♡ A Q 2 ◇ A K 6 4 ♣ A Q 5

Superficial reasoning would go like this: "I have 24 points; all I need from partner is 2 measly points to give us the magic total of 26 for game. Surely he has 2 points of the 16 that are missing. If, by chance, he is completely broke, I'll pay off—or play the hand like a wizard to make it anyway. So here goes: *'Three notrump.'*"

Now let's see what your expectancy is opposite one key honor card in partner's hand:

PARTNER'S HOLDING	NUMBER OF TRICKS YOU CAN EXPECT TO TAKE
♠ A, A x or A x x	$7^{1}/_{2}$
♠ A x x x	$7^{13}/_{16}$
♡ or ♣ K, K x or K x x	$7^{1}/_{2}$
♡ or ♣ K x x x	$7^{13}/_{16}$
◇ Q or Q x	$6^{1}/_{2}$
◇ Q x x	$6^{13}/_{16}$
◇ Q x x x	$7^{7}/_{16}$

Purists, please note: this chart takes into account the chance the suit will break favorably for an extra trick. Furthermore, we assume that when diamonds break 3–2, dummy's Q x x x will provide two entries for finesses.

Perhaps your left-hand opponent will give you a free finesse on the opening lead. But if he is not that generous, better refrain from bellowing three notrump: for you have barely a whisper of a prayer to land nine tricks.

The truth is that you need *more* than 26 points for game when one hand holds the preponderance of strength. The extra margin makes up for the lack of transportation facilities to dummy. If you hold 24 points, even 4 points opposite may not give you a good play for game. Now we can get down to the requirements for an opening three-notrump bid:

1. A point count of 24 points, provided you can count eight tricks in your own hand, *or* a point count of 25–27.

2. Balanced distribution: 4–3–3–3, 4–4–3–2 or 5–3–3–2 (the last only if the 5-card suit is a minor).

3. Stoppers in all four suits.

Try your skill on the following hands:

(1) ♠ A K ♡ A K Q ◇ A K 8 2 ♣ Q 7 6 4. *Bid three notrump.* 25 points, balanced distribution, stoppers in all four suits.

(2) ♠ A J 10 ♡ A Q ◇ A K 8 6 4 ♣ A Q 5. *Bid three notrump.* 25 points, including 1 point for the fifth diamond.

(3) ♠ K Q J 10 ♡ A K Q ◇ A 7 5 ♣ K Q 7. *Bid three notrump.* 24 points, but you can count eight tricks in your own hand.

(4) ♠ A K J ♡ K Q 8 6 ◇ A K 10 ♣ K J 10. *Bid two notrump.* 24 points, but only six sure tricks in your own hand. It's better to view the hand as 24– points and open just two notrump.

RESPONSES TO THREE NOTRUMP

Responder passes three notrump unless he wishes to make a slam try or feels the hand will play better in a suit. Here is a rundown of the various bids at his disposal and their meanings:

Pass: Not enough points to try for slam; responder's hand is sufficiently balanced to be content with notrump.

Four hearts or four spades: Preference for a suit contract, based on a 6-card suit no better than K J x x x.

Four diamonds: Preference for a five-diamond contract, based on a 7-card suit with a queen somewhere in the hand (may be outside the trump suit).

Four clubs: Stayman, looking for a 4–4 major suit fit. Opener should not construe this as a slam try, but only as a search for a better contract. If responder has slam aspirations, it will come out on his next bid.

Raises in notrump: Slam tries as follows:

NUMBER OF POINTS RESPONDER HOLDS	RESPONDER'S BID OVER PARTNER'S 3NT
7	4NT
8	4♣ (Stayman), then 4NT over partner's response
9	5NT
10	4♣, then 5NT
11	6NT
12	4♣, then 6NT
13 and over	7NT

Just remember that the table starts at 7 points and progresses 1 point at a time. (Once every ten years you might miss a slam when partner has a maximum 27 opposite your 6, but more often than not, the imbalance between the hands and the communication problems it causes would doom such a slam.)

Opener adds his points to those shown by partner's raise and places the final contract—at six notrump if the assets total 33–36 points, at seven notrump if they total 37 or over.

Here are a few sample hands to bid after partner has opened three notrump:

(1) ♠ 9 8 4 ♡ 10 9 6 5 ◇ Q 8 7 ♣ 6 5 3. *Pass.* Your lone queen probably won't be enough to bring home game, but there is no better spot. Even if partner has four hearts, there is no reason to think a four-heart contract will play any better.

(2) ♠ K 7 3 ♡ Q 5 4 ◇ 8 7 6 2 ♣ 10 6 5. *Pass.* This time partner should be a shoo-in for three notrump, but since there is no chance for slam, there is also no reason to disturb a winning contract.

(3) ♠ 5 ♡ 9 7 6 4 3 2 ◇ Q 6 4 ♣ 8 5 3. *Bid four hearts.* A 6-card suit and a side queen, exactly what the bid requires.

(4) ♠ Q 8 6 5 4 3 ♡ 8 3 ◇ 9 5 2 ♣ 9 3. *Bid four spades.* The same situation, except this time the queen is in your long suit. If you were tempted to pass, look at partner's hand: ♠ A J 9 ♡ A K J ◇ K Q J ♣ K Q J 6. Unless the opponents get a ruff, four spades should roll. But at three notrump if either opponent holds K x x (or K x x x) in spades and holds up his king, partner will have a rough time making his bid. And mind you, the odds are 4 to 3 that you'll find the spade king twice guarded.

(5) ♠ K Q 5 ♡ Q 10 6 ◇ K Q 6 2 ♣ 7 3 2. *Bid four clubs and follow with six notrump.* Again, the book bid, with 12 points, but we put this hand in just in case you were wondering when to bid a grand slam. Doesn't 12 + 25 = 37, enough for a grand slam? Yes, but partner's hand may include a point for distribution, e.g.: ♠ A J ♡ K J 9 ◇ A J 5 ♣ A K Q J 8. You have 37 points together, all right, yet there are 4 points outstanding. The fact that they are all gathered together in the ace of hearts is your tough luck, and you'll have a jolly time explaining your "odds-on" grand slam bid to an irate partner.

(6) ♠ Q 8 7 3 ♡ 10 5 4 2 ◇ 10 7 6 3 ♣ 6. *Bid four clubs, Stayman.* Your 2 points won't help a three-notrump contract much, but four of a major has an excellent chance.

(7) ♠ Q 8 7 3 ♡ Q 5 4 2 ◇ 10 6 3 ♣ 7 6. *Pass.* Four of a major may be a better contract, but you are out in the cold if partner doesn't have a 4-card major. Your two queens should be all he needs to make three notrump, so this is not the time for high adventure. Pass when you are in an adequate contract; bid only when you have really good prospects of improving an inadequate contract.

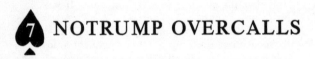 NOTRUMP OVERCALLS

WHEN YOU ARE dealer and your hand calls for a one-notrump bid, nobody can beat you to the punch. The rules of the game stipulate that the dealer is the first to speak. But you get the deal only one-fourth of the time. Thus many times during your bridge career an inconsiderate opponent will open the bidding ahead of you just when you were all set to bid one notrump. What to do? Should you bid one notrump anyway or double or overcall or pass? In this chapter we will evaluate the pros and cons of each alternative.

THE IMMEDIATE OVERCALL OF ONE NOTRUMP

The requirements for an immediate *overcall* of one notrump are basically the same as for an *opening* one-notrump bid—balanced distribution, 16–18 points, stoppers in three suits. But pay special attention to your holding in opener's suit.

Remember the opening bid has given the opponents a head start in planning their defense against your notrump contract: the opponent on your left has been alerted to lead his partner's suit; the opening bidder is marked with some side strength with which to regain the lead to keep punching away at his suit. Therefore, you need that much extra to ward off the attack.

Certainly you need one sure stopper in the suit. We go one step further and avoid a notrump overcall on 16 points unless we have a *double* stopper. In effect, a double stopper raises the point count of the hand to 17 or 18, since its favorable location behind the bidder upgrades the honors.

DON'T STRETCH

One of the surest ways to lose a bundle is to shade your requirements for a notrump overcall. Some 15-point hands look very inviting, but you must restrain the impulse to overcall one notrump. It is too easy for your left-hand opponent to inflict a punishing double. Everybody at the table knows that the opening bid and the notrump overcall account for almost three-quarters of the high-card strength in the deck. When your left-hand opponent has the balance, he will be only too happy to double. Perhaps you will find an escape suit at the two level; perhaps not. But you are sure to find a nearly worthless dummy. You can't get rich playing one notrump doubled out of your hand when you have but 15 points.

ALTERNATE ACTIONS

The requirements for an opening one-notrump bid are quite rigid. Those for an immediate notrump overcall, even more so. When your hand does not qualify for a notrump overcall, there are still several choices available to you:

1. *Takeout double:* This is the preferred action when you lack a stopper in the opponent's suit, and have a 4-card holding in at least one unbid major suit.

2. *Overcall in a suit:* If you have a good 5-card suit, an overcall is the logical action. Even a strong 4-card suit will suffice for an overcall at the one level.

3. *Pass:* This is one of the most valuable and money-saving calls at bridge. Call it a trap pass, if you will, or admit to yourself that no other action is worth the risk. Chances are you will get another and safer opportunity to bid—when more is known about the opponents' hands. But if you decide to pass, do it quickly. If you agonize over your decision, the opponents will get the message and adjust their tactics accordingly. And remember a "slow pass" puts your partner in an uncomfortable position; he too knows you have "tickets" but bridge proprieties require that he bend over backward to avoid using information to which he is not entitled.

SAMPLE HANDS

The bidding has gone:

EAST	SOUTH
1♡	?

and you, South, hold:

(1) ♠ A Q 6 ♡ K 7 4 ◊ J 8 6 2 ♣ A K 8. *Bid one notrump.* 17 points, balanced distribution, a stopper in the opponent's suit.

(2) ♠ Q J 4 ♡ K J 6 ◊ A Q 10 9 ♣ K 9 5. *Bid one notrump.* The hand counts to only 16 high-card points, but a double stopper in the opponent's suit makes the real point count higher.

(3) ♠ K 5 4 ♡ K Q 10 ◊ K 6 ♣ A Q 10 7 4. *Double,* then bid no-trump at your next turn. This hand is just a shade too good for a no-trump overcall. You have 17 high-card points, but should add 1 point for the fifth club and 1 for the excellent double stopper in the opponent's suit—for a total of 19.

(4) ♠ A Q 9 8 ♡ 8 6 5 ◊ A K ♣ Q J 8 4. *Double.* No stopper in the bid suit and only 16 points. With a good 4-card holding in the other major, a takeout double is the logical action.

(5) ♠ A Q 8 ♡ 9 7 6 5 ◊ A K ♣ A J 10 8. *Bid one notrump.* This contradicts our previous injunction about requiring a stopper in the bid suit for a notrump overcall, but the hand is too powerful to pass and there is no other reasonable action except the no-trump overcall. As compensation for the missing heart stopper, you have 18 points and four cards in the opponent's suit. In large part, winning bidding technique is a matter of selecting the least awkward action when faced with a choice of evils. (After all, few players need guidance when one standout bid ideally describes the hand.)

(6) ♠ K 5 ♡ 8 5 4 ◊ A 9 5 ♣ A K Q 10 6. *Bid two clubs.* This spotlights the major strength of your hand and marks a lead if the opponents buy the contract. Moreover, your bid makes it more difficult for the opponents to proceed with their bidding. In any event, you do not want to overcall with one notrump without a heart stopper as long as you have a reasonable alternative.

(7) ♠ A Q ♡ 7 5 4 ◊ A Q 6 5 ♣ K J 8 4. *Pass.* By process of elim-ination, this is the only sensible course; you can't bid one no-trump with 16 points missing a stopper in the adverse suit; it is unwise to double with only doubleton support in the other major; and your minor suits are too ragged and short to risk an overcall at the two level. So you have to pass for the moment. It may not be a "cheerful" pass, but don't feel too glum about it, for you may get a chance to speak up later—perhaps with a resounding penalty double after the opponents get up too high.

RESPONSES TO
A ONE-NOTRUMP OVERCALL

The responses to a one-notrump overcall are exactly the same as the responses to an opening one-notrump bid except that one new bid is available —the cue-bid in the opponent's suit. This is a stronger version of the Stayman two-club response, and is forcing to game. Of course, a two-club response remains on tap as the versatile Stayman bid, inquiring about major suits. There is one ambiguous requence:

EAST	SOUTH	WEST	NORTH
1♣	1NT	Pass	2♣

North's bid should be interpreted as Stayman, not as a cue-bid. This construction allows North to look for either a game or a playable part-score. If we viewed two clubs as a cue-bid, forcing to game, we would deprive North of a valuable tool for part-score exploration.

A considerable amount of judgment is required to weigh the effect of the opening bid. Responder should recognize that the opening lead will probably be in the opponent's bid suit; if he holds a weak doubleton or singleton in that suit, he should think about a suit contract. On the other hand, the opener's partner can have very little strength and is unlikely to regain the lead. Therefore, a holding like Q x x in the opponent's suit acts almost as a sure stopper. Likewise, holdings like Q J x or J 10 x in side suits figure to be worth more than they appear, for they provide material with which to finesse through the strong hand. You have a great advantage during the play when you know which opponent has the bulk of the outstanding strength. If the bidding tells you that your cards are well placed in relation to the strong opponent, you should be more bullish in looking for game.

REOPENING THE BIDDING

When the opening suit bid has been followed by two passes, the last man to speak often has a difficult decision. Should he reopen the bidding? If so, how? Here is the typical sequence:

WEST	NORTH	EAST	SOUTH
1♡	Pass	Pass	?

Let's start with East, as his hand is the easiest to dope out: East has less than 6 points or he would have kept the bidding open. West's hand is a bit tougher to figure; in standard American methods an opening bid of one in a suit has a wide range. West could have as few as 11 points or as many as 22. For the sake of simplicity, let's credit him with 14 points for his opening bid. Thus East-

West presumably have no more than 19 points between them. This means your side has better than half the deck and some action is called for.

The big mystery man in this little drama is your partner, North. Say you have 10 points. Then he probably has over 10 himself. It is surely cowardly to pass in South's position when the hand probably belongs to you. But how far do you go to "protect" your partner? This is one of the most controversial questions in the theory of bridge bidding. Articles, books, monographs and sheer nonsense have been written on the subject. It is beyond the scope of this book to analyze all the factors. But one overriding truth stands out: the criteria for reopening the bidding in fourth position can only have meaning in relation to the partnership philosophy on immediate overcalls. If North doesn't believe in light overcalls, or if he likes to make trap passes at every opportunity, then South has to lean over backward to "protect" his partner. If North is not chary of bidding his values, then there is less reason for South to overcompensate. Our own feeling is that "protection" is generally overdone; we feel a bit uncomfortable with a bidding philosophy that requires one partner to overextend himself to bid the other's hand for him.

DOUBLE FIRST WITH A STRONG NOTRUMP HAND

All of the foregoing serves as introduction for handling notrump hands in the reopening position. On full-strength hands—those which you would have opened one notrump in first position—double first and then bid notrump at the minimum level on your next turn. This ties in with the general rule of reopening: A double shows real values—enough to come into the bidding in any position. The one exception is a jump to two notrump. Conventionally, this announces the values for an opening notrump call—16–18 points—but with weakness in the unbid major suit. Before using this construction, better discuss it with your favorite partner, for many players interpret a notrump jump in this position as the "unusual notrump" convention, asking for partner's better minor suit.

The first usage has two advantages: (1) it enables the partnership to distinguish between two types of hands ordinarily opened with one notrump, thereby reducing the head start the opponents gained when they opened the bidding; (2) it tells the whole story of the hand in one bid, preventing the opener's partner from effectively obstructing the bidding.

Besides, there is no real need for the "unusual notrump" convention here. If fourth hand has a two-suited rockcrusher, he can cue-bid the opponent's suit to force to game and later bid both his minor suits. With lesser strength he can overcall in one minor, and bid the other later, if he gets the chance. If his partner doesn't have enough to keep the bidding open so he can show his second suit, then it is unlikely that the pair have missed a game.

SHADE THE NOTRUMP OVERCALL

Since a double shows a good hand, a nonjump notrump overcall in the reopening position naturally promises less—anywhere from 11 to 14 points. Generally, a good part of the strength is in the opponent's suit. Ideally, this call shows a double stopper in the suit, but a notrump overcall is the best choice on many hands with a single stop and outside compensation.

DOUBLE WITH INTEREST IN THE MAJORS

A notrump overcall implies strength in the opponent's suit and inadequate support for the unbid major suit(s). A takeout double states just the opposite: shortness in the bid suit and support for the unbid major(s). Of course, there will be an overlap—hands that qualify for a one-notrump overcall which have good 4-card support for one of the majors. Our advice is to bid one notrump if the hand truly qualifies and has no flaws, such as only a single stopper in the opponent's suit or one unstopped side suit. Otherwise, double for takeout. However, in the latter case, you have to look ahead. If partner happens to respond in your weakest suit, you will have to pass quietly. You should not rebid in notrump, for that would indicate 16–18 points, as explained above.

SAMPLE HANDS

The bidding has been:

WEST	NORTH	EAST	SOUTH
1♡	Pass	Pass	?

and you, South, hold:

(1) ♠ Q 7 5 ♡ K J 8 3 ◇ A Q ♣ J 10 7 4. *Bid one notrump.* A balanced hand of 13 high-card points including a double stop in the opponent's suit.

(2) ♠ A Q 3 ♡ K 10 9 ◇ A 10 9 ♣ J 10 9 3. *Bid one notrump.* As compensation for a single stopper in the enemy suit, you have a maximum 14 points and a profusion of tens and nines that may come in handy.

(3) ♠ Q 6 4 ♡ K Q 10 5 4 ◇ K 7 ♣ A 5 3. *Pass.* When you have length in the opponent's suit, a pass figures to work out best. You will probably defeat one heart and earn a plus score, and yet there is little likelihood that your partner has enough for game. Partner is surely short in hearts and your heart strength won't fit his hand. Furthermore, your own heart holding tells you that partner probably has not made a trap pass, for that is usually based on a good holding in the opponent's suit. Fortunately, for you, West has hit upon a suit that is stacked against him. Let him stay fixed; any bid

by you will give him a chance to extricate himself. If it turns out that East-West have no suit fit, chances are that your side doesn't either, which is still another reason to let West suffer at one heart. Lastly, if you bid one notrump and are allowed to play there, you'd feel pretty silly if West has a two suiter and beats your brains out with his second suit. In all, quite a convincing case for passing gracefully and accepting a small profit.

(4) ♠ A Q 7 5 ♡ K 7 5 ◇ A 8 ♣ J 10 8 7. *Double.* When you have four cards in the higher-ranking major suit, double unless you have an ideal notrump. Here the single heart stopper tips the scale in favor of the double.

RESPONDING TO A REOPENING
ONE–NOTRUMP OVERCALL

Responder needs judgment and discipline when he hears his partner reopen with one notrump: judgment, because there may be a game in the hand if his cards are well placed; discipline, because the bidding can easily get out of hand if he forgets partner's strength is strictly limited.

Whenever the opponents get into the bidding first, it becomes more difficult to bid to the optimum contract, and adjustments are called for. In the case of a reopening notrump, the Stayman two-club bid becomes more flexible if it is used in a nonforcing sense: Thus, in this sequence:

WEST	NORTH	EAST	SOUTH
1♡	Pass	Pass	1NT
Pass	2♣	Pass	2◇
Pass	2♠	Pass	?

South should pass unless he has a maximum and an excellent spade fit. North's bidding does not imply any interest in game. If he wanted to reach game, he could use one of three different bidding sequences:

	WEST	NORTH	EAST	SOUTH
(1)	1♡	Pass	Pass	1NT
	Pass	2♡		
(2)	1♡	Pass	Pass	1NT
	Pass	2♣	Pass	2◇
	Pass	3♠		
(3)	1♡	Pass	Pass	1NT
	Pass	3♠		

Sequence (1) illustrates the cue-bid, ordinarily based on a 12-point hand or a slightly weaker hand with compensating distributional advantages. Sequences (2) and (3) must be game forces, since they are both jumps to the three level in a major suit. In (2) North chose to use Stayman en route, for reasons of his own, but the ultimate meaning is the same.

A simple takeout to two of a new suit remains a weak bid and partner is expected to pass, viz.:

WEST	NORTH	EAST	SOUTH
1♢	Pass	Pass	1NT
Pass	2♡ (or 2♠)	Pass	?

South needs compelling reasons to make any other bid but a pass.

SAMPLE HANDS

The bidding has progressed:

WEST	NORTH	EAST	SOUTH
1♠	Pass	Pass	1NT
Pass	?		

and you, North, hold:

(1) ♠ 8 4 ♡ Q J 10 6 2 ♢ K Q 7 5 ♣ Q 4. *Bid two hearts.* This figures to be a better contract than one notrump, and game is chancy at best, for partner may have only 11 points and a poor heart fit. If partner does make another bid, showing a maximum hand and a good heart fit, you should be delighted to bid the game.

(2) ♠ 7 ♡ Q 6 5 4 3 2 ♢ A Q 10 ♣ Q 6 4. *Bid two spades.* The cue-bid is a game force, and you can show your hearts at your next turn. Alternatively, you could bid two clubs, Stayman, and then jump in hearts; or you could bid three hearts immediately. The important thing is to recognize you have a good hand—10 high-card points, a 6-card major suit and a singleton in the opponent's suit—and to make sure of getting to game.

The bidding has gone:

WEST	NORTH	EAST	SOUTH
1♢	Pass	Pass	1NT
Pass	?		

and you, North, hold:

(1) ♠ K J 8 2 ♡ 8 7 6 4 2 ♢ 6 4 ♣ A 5. *Bid two clubs, Stayman.* You will pass whichever major suit partner bids and land in a better spot than one notrump. If South responds two diamonds, correct to two hearts, which partner will usually pass.

SUMMARY—

MEANING OF BIDS

(PART I)

THE NEXT TWELVE PAGES are a recap of the meaning of various bids—and sequences—included in Part I. It is intended as a refresher, as well as a handy checklist for reference when a question arises.

In each case the comment applies to the last bid in the sequence, which is underlined. Of course, the full message is conditioned by the previous bidding. Unless otherwise noted, the opponents have not entered the bidding, nor has partner passed.

There is no attempt to cover all possible bidding sequences. That would take a book in itself. But with the wide range of situations shown, common sense will do the trick for any that are missing. Where there is any real chance for ambiguity, we have included a sequence even though it may not be specifically mentioned in the text.

1. OPENING BID OF ONE NOTRUMP:

OPENER
1NT   16–18 points, balanced distribution, stoppers in at least three suits, no 5-card major as good as K J x x x.

2. STAYMAN CONVENTION:

SOUTH   NORTH
1NT   2♣   Stayman Convention, asking partner to name a biddable 4-card major suit (Q x x x or better) if he has one.

3. OPENER'S REBIDS TO THE STAYMAN TWO–CLUB BID:

	SOUTH	NORTH	
(1)	1NT	2♣	Biddable 4-card spade suit (Q x x x or
	2♠		better), may also have biddable 4-card
			heart suit.

	SOUTH	NORTH	
(2)	1NT	2♣	Biddable 4-card heart suit (Q x x x or
	2♡		better), no biddable 4-card spade suit.

	SOUTH	NORTH	
(3)	1NT	2♣	No biddable 4-card major suit.
	2◇		

4. RESPONSES TO AN OPENING ONE–NOTRUMP BID

A. There is no game when responder has 7 points or less:

	SOUTH	NORTH	
(1)	1NT	*Pass*	No preference for a suit contract.

	SOUTH	NORTH	
(2)	1NT	*2◇ , 2♡*	Correction to a better contract on an
		or 2♠	unbalanced hand, at least a 5-card
			suit.

	SOUTH	NORTH	
(3)	1NT	*3♣ or 3◇*	Pre-emptive bid, 6- or 7-card suit.

	SOUTH	NORTH	
(4)	1NT	*2♣*	Stayman Convention, asking if part-
			ner has a biddable 4-card major suit;
			North plans to pass South's rebid.

	SOUTH	NORTH	
(5)	1NT	2♣	Finding a better part-score than one
	2◇ , 2♡	*Pass*	notrump.
	or 2♠		

B. Responder invites game with 8–9 points:

	SOUTH	NORTH	
(1)	1NT	*2NT*	No interest in a major-suit contract,
			usually a balanced hand. South can
			pass.

	SOUTH	NORTH
(2)	1NT	*2♣*

Stayman Convention, asking if partner has 4-card biddable major suit; North plans to rebid.

	SOUTH	NORTH
(3)	1NT	2♣
	2◊ or 2♡	*2NT*

South has not bid North's 4-card major. South may now pass.

	SOUTH	NORTH
(4)	1NT	2♣
	2♠	*2NT*

4- or 5-card heart suit. South will now bid hearts if he has four of them. But South can pass if he lacks four hearts.

	SOUTH	NORTH
(5)	1NT	2♣
	2♡	*3♡*

4- or 5-card suit. South can pass.

C. *Responder makes sure of getting to game with 10 points or more:*

	SOUTH	NORTH
(1)	1NT	*3NT*

No interest in a major-suit contract, usually a balanced hand. South must pass.

	SOUTH	NORTH
(2)	1NT	*4♡ or 4♠*

6-card or good 5-card suit. Ten-point minimum may include distributional points. South must pass.

	SOUTH	NORTH
(3)	1NT	*2♣*

Stayman Convention, asking if partner has 4-card biddable major suit; North will make a forcing rebid.

	SOUTH	NORTH
(4)	1NT	2♣
	2♠	*4♠*
or	1NT	2♣
	2♡	*4♡*

4- or 5- card support. South must pass.

	SOUTH	NORTH
(5)	1NT	2♣
	2◊ or 2♡	*3NT*

Four (but not five) spades. South must pass.

	SOUTH	NORTH
(6)	1NT	2♣
	2♠	*3NT*

Four cards in hearts. South corrects to four hearts if he too has four cards in the suit. Otherwise he passes.

	SOUTH	NORTH
(7)	1NT	2♣
	2♠	*3♡*
or	1NT	*3♡ or 3♠*

Five-card suit, asking for a raise on 3-card support. Forcing to game.

	SOUTH	NORTH
(8)	1NT	2♣
	2◇ , 2♡	*3♣ or 3◇*
	or 2♠	

Length or strength in the suit bid, asks South for more information, forcing.

D. Responder forces another bid from opener. It is not yet clear whether he wants to invite game or insist upon it:

	SOUTH	NORTH
	1NT	2♣
	2◇ or 2♡	*2♠*
or	1NT	2♣
	2◇	*2♡*

5-card or longer suit. South must raise with 3-card support, jumping to game with a maximum, raising to three otherwise. Without 3-card support, South bids three notrump with a maximum, two notrump with less. North will pass South's rebid with 8–9 points, but will raise to game with 10 or more, unless South has already bid game.

E. Responder looks for slam (holding 14 points or more):

	SOUTH	NORTH
(1)	1NT	*2♣*

Unbalanced hand—Stayman Convention, asking partner to name a biddable 4-card major suit if he has one; North plans to make further forcing bid(s) until game, at least, is reached.

	SOUTH	NORTH
(2)	1NT	*4NT*

Balanced hand—15 points.

	SOUTH	NORTH	
(3)	1NT	2♣	Balanced hand—16 points.
	2◇, 2♡	*4NT*	
	or 2♠		

	SOUTH	NORTH	
(4)	1NT	*5NT*	Balanced hand—17 points.

	SOUTH	NORTH	
(5)	1NT	2♣	Balanced hand—18 points.
	2◇, 2♡	*5NT*	
	or 2♠		

	SOUTH	NORTH	
(6)	1NT	*6NT*	Balanced hand—19 points.

	SOUTH	NORTH	
(7)	1NT	2♣	Balanced hand—20 points.
	2◇, 2♡	*6NT*	
	or 2♠		

	SOUTH	NORTH	
(8)	1NT	*7NT*	Balanced hand—21 points.

5. OPENER'S REBIDS

A. *Opener declines responder's game invitation when he holds a minimum:*

SOUTH	NORTH
1NT	2♣
2♡	2NT or 3♡
Pass	

or 1NT	NORTH
1NT	2♣
2♠	2NT or 3♠
Pass	

or 1NT	NORTH
1NT	2NT
Pass	

B. *Opener must accept responder's choice of game contract:*

SOUTH	NORTH
1NT	2♣
2♡	4♡
Pass	

or 1NT 2♣
  2♠ 4♣
  Pass

or 1NT 3NT
  Pass

or 1NT 4♡ or 4♠
  Pass

C. *Opener, holding both majors, corrects to hearts:*

	SOUTH	NORTH	
(1)	1NT	2♣	South has four hearts, knows responder
	2♠	3NT	also has four hearts, therefore chooses
	4♡		the superior game contract.

	SOUTH	NORTH	
(2)	1NT	2♣	South has four hearts and a minimum
	2♠	2NT	notrump. (With better than a mini-
	3♡		mum, he'd bid four hearts.)

D. *Opener has a minimum, but must reply to partner's forcing rebid:*

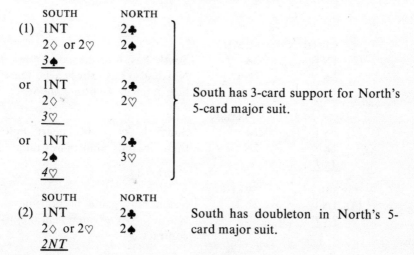

	SOUTH	NORTH	
(1)	1NT	2♣	
	2◇ or 2♡	2♠	
	3♠		
or	1NT	2♣	South has 3-card support for North's
	2◇	2♡	5-card major suit.
	3♡		
or	1NT	2♣	
	2♠	3♡	
	4♡		

	SOUTH	NORTH	
(2)	1NT	2♣	South has doubleton in North's 5-
	2◇ or 2♡	2♠	card major suit.
	2NT		

or 1NT	2♣	
2◇	2♡	
2NT		South has a doubleton in North's 5-card major suit.
or 1NT	2♣	
2♠	3♡	
3NT		

	SOUTH	NORTH	
(3)	1NT	2♣	South has stoppers in the three unbid suits, or a minimum hand with a doubtful stopper.
	2◇ , 2♡	3♣ or 3◇	
	or 2♠		
	3NT		

	SOUTH	NORTH	
(4)	1NT	2♣	South lacks a stopper in one suit (disregarding the suit just bid by North), bids his *strongest* suit to guide North.
	2◇ , 2♡	3♣ or 3◇	
	or 2♠		
	3♡ or 3♠		

E. *Opener accepts partner's game invitation with better than a minimum:*

	SOUTH	NORTH	
(1)	1NT	2♣	
	2♠	3♠	
	4♠		
or	1NT	2♣	Bidding game in the agreed suit.
	2♡	3♡	
	4♡		

	SOUTH	NORTH	
(2)	1NT	2♣	South has four hearts, knows that North also has four hearts, therefore bids game in the fitting major.
	2♠	2NT	
	4♡		

	SOUTH	NORTH	
(3)	1NT	2♣	South lacks 4-card heart holding, therefore bids game in notrump.
	2♠	2NT	
	3NT		

	SOUTH	NORTH	
(4)	1NT	2NT	South bids game in notrump after North shows no interest in major-suit contract.
	3NT		

6. INTERFERENCE AFTER AN OPENING NOTRUMP

A. *Action by the notrumper's partner:*

	SOUTH	WEST	NORTH
(1)	1NT	2♡	***2♠ , 3♣*** *or 3♢*

Competitive, limited, nonforcing. At least a 5-card suit, probably less than 8 points.

	SOUTH	WEST	NORTH
(2)	1NT	2♠	*3♡*
or	1NT	2♡	*3♠*

} 5-card suit, game force. South raises with 3-card support, otherwise rebids three notrump.

	SOUTH	WEST	NORTH
(3)	1NT	2♢	*3♢*

Cue-bid, force to game. South is asked to name an unbid 4-card major.

B. *Opener's rebid:*

	SOUTH	WEST	NORTH	EAST
(1)	1NT *3♡*	2♢	2♡	Pass

Pre-emptive, not invitational.

	SOUTH	WEST	NORTH	EAST
(2)	1NT	2♢	2♡	2♠ , 3♣ or 3♢
	3♡			
or	1NT *4♢*	2♠	3♢	3♠

} Continuing the competition, nonforcing.

	SOUTH	WEST	NORTH	EAST
(3)	1NT *2♠* *or 3♣*	2♢	2♡	Pass

Game invitation, one-round force. Four-card trump support, maximum notrump, strength in bid suit.

	SOUTH	WEST	NORTH	EAST
(4)	1NT *3♢*	2♢	2♡	Pass

Game invitation, one-round force. Fine fit with North's suit, a maximum notrump, stopper in opponent's suit, suggesting a notrump game.

7. HANDS TOO STRONG FOR AN OPENING ONE-NOTRUMP BID

A.   Opener's action:

OPENER

(1) *2NT*   21+ to 24– points, balanced hand, stoppers in all four suits.

OPENER

(2) *3NT*   24-27 points, balanced hand, stoppers in all four suits.

	SOUTH	NORTH
(3)	1♣	1♡
	2NT	
or	1♠	2♡
	3NT	

18+ to 20– points, balanced hand, stoppers in all but partner's suit.

	SOUTH	NORTH
(4)	1♣	1♡
	2NT	

20+ to 21– points, balanced hand, stoppers in all but partner's suit.

B.   Responder's action:

	SOUTH	NORTH
(1)	2NT	*3NT*

5-10 points, hand suitable for no-trump, no slam interest.

	SOUTH	NORTH
(2)	2NT	*3♣*

Stayman Convention, asking for biddable 4-card major suit.

	SOUTH	NORTH
(3)	2NT	*3◇ , 3♡*
		or *3♠*

5-card suit, game force. South will raise major with good 3-card support.

	SOUTH	NORTH
(4)	2NT	*4♡ or 4♠*

6-card suit, unbalanced hand, unsuited for notrump, no slam interest.

	SOUTH	NORTH
(5)	3NT	*4♣*

Stayman, asking for 4-card biddable major suit.

	SOUTH	NORTH	
(6)	3NT	_4◇_	Prefers diamond contract, 7-card suit, game force.

	SOUTH	NORTH	
(7)	3NT	_4♡ or 4♠_	6-card suit, but no better than K J x x x x. Not a slam try.

	SOUTH	NORTH	
(8)	1♡	1♠	Sign-off. North wants to play at three
	2NT	_3♠_	spades.

	SOUTH	NORTH	
(9)	1◇	1♡	Forward-going, natural bid, forcing
	2NT	_3♣, 3◇_	to game (three clubs is *not* Stayman).
		_or 3♠_	

8. NOTRUMP OVERCALLS

A.   The immediate notrump overcall:

	EAST	SOUTH	
	1♣, 1◇,	_1NT_	16–18 points, stoppers in three suits,
	1♡ or 1♠		including opponent's (double stopper if only 16 points).

B.   Responses to the immediate notrump overcall:

	EAST	SOUTH	WEST	NORTH	
(1)	1◇	1NT	Pass	_2◇_	Cue-bid, force to game, asks
or	1♡	1NT	Pass	_2♡_	South for biddable 4-card major
or	1♠	1NT	Pass	_2♠_	suit.

	EAST	SOUTH	WEST	NORTH	
(2)	1♣, 1◇, 1NT		Pass	_2♣_	Stayman, asking South for bid-
	1♡ or 1♠				dable 4-card major suit.

	EAST	SOUTH	WEST	NORTH	
(3)	1♣, 1◇, 1NT		Pass	_Pass_	No preference for suit contract,
	1♡ or 1♠				7 points or less.

	EAST	SOUTH	WEST	NORTH	
(4)	1♣	1NT	Pass	_2◇, 2♡_	5-card suit, 7 points or less, wants
				_or 2♠_	South to pass, not forcing.

EAST	SOUTH	WEST	NORTH	
(5) 1♡	1NT	Pass	*3♣*	Pre-emptive bid, 6- or 7- card
or 1♠			or *3◇*	suit.

EAST	SOUTH	WEST	NORTH	
(6) 1♣, 1◇, 1NT	Pass		*2NT*	8–9 points, game invitation, no
1♡ or 1♠				major-suit interest.

EAST	SOUTH	WEST	NORTH	
(7) 1♣	1NT	Pass	*3♡*	5-card suit, asking for raise on
or 1◇			or *3♠*	3-card support. Forcing to game.

EAST	SOUTH	WEST	NORTH	
(8) 1♣, 1◇, 1NT	Pass		*4♠*	6-card or good 5-card suit. Min-
or 1♡				imum of 10 points (may include
				distributional points). South
				must pass.

EAST	SOUTH	WEST	NORTH	
(9) 1♣, 1◇, 1NT	Pass		*3NT*	No interest in major suits. At
1♡ or 1♠				least 10 points.

C. *Reopening actions:*

WEST	NORTH	EAST	SOUTH	
(1) 1♣, 1◇, Pass		Pass	*1NT*	11–14 points, balanced, generally
1♡ or 1♠				good part of strength in op-
				ponent's suit (ideally a double
				stopper).

WEST	NORTH	EAST	SOUTH	
(2) 1♣, 1◇, Pass		Pass	*Double*	Values for an opening bid, gen-
1♡ or 1♠				erally short in opponent's suit,
				interest in unbid major(s).

WEST	NORTH	EAST	SOUTH	
(3) 1♣, 1◇	Pass	Pass	Double	16–18 points, balanced hand,
or 1♡				stoppers in all unbid suits (in-
Pass	1♠	Pass	*1NT*	cluding opponent's), tolerance
or 1♡, 1♠	Pass	Pass	Double	for unbid majors.
Pass	2◇	Pass	*2NT*	

WEST	NORTH	EAST	SOUTH
(4) 1♣, 1♢, Pass	Pass		*2NT*
1♡ or 1♠			

16–18 points, balanced hand, stoppers in three suits (including opponent's), weak in unbid major(s).

D. Responses to reopening actions:

WEST	NORTH	EAST	SOUTH
(1) 1♢, 1♡	Pass	Pass	1NT
or 1♠			
Pass	*2♣*		

Stayman, asks for South's 4-card major suit. Non-forcing. (South may pass if North rebids two of unbid major.)

WEST	NORTH	EAST	SOUTH
(2) 1♢	Pass	Pass	1NT
Pass	2♣	Pass	2♢
Pass	*2♡ or 2♠*		

Not forcing, no real interest in game. South should pass unless he has both maximum and excellent fit.

WEST	NORTH	EAST	SOUTH
(3) 1♢	Pass	Pass	1NT
Pass	2♣	Pass	2♢
			or 2♡
Pass	*3♠*		
or 1♢	Pass	Pass	1NT
Pass	*3♡ or 3♠*		

Game force, 12 points or more, asks for raise on 3-card support, otherwise three-notrump rebid. Shows at least 5-card suit.

WEST	NORTH	EAST	SOUTH
(4) 1♡	Pass	Pass	1NT
Pass	*2♡*		

Cue-bid, forcing to game, 12 points minimum (approximately), asks for South's 4-card major suit.

WEST	NORTH	EAST	SOUTH
(5) 1♡	Pass	Pass	1NT
Pass	*2♢ or 2♠*		

Correction to better contract, 5-card or better suit, 11 points or less, not forcing.

WEST	NORTH	EAST	SOUTH
(6) 1♣, 1♢, Pass	Pass		1NT
1♡ or 1♠			
Pass	*2NT*		

Game invitation, balanced hand, no interest in suit contract, approximately 12 points.

PART TWO

for

ADVANCED
PLAYERS

INTRODUCTION

TO ADVANCED SECTION

BY THIS TIME you should be an old pro at notrump. Well, enough of a pro to take care of the boys at your club game.

But bridge is played at many levels: as a game of skill, it has almost infinite potential. Every redblooded player will want to go as far as his aptitude will take him—just as in the game of life, itself.

However, even the most expert player cannot "go it alone." Bridge is a partnership game. Our aim therefore is to *expand* the language of bidding to establish an intelligent dialogue between advanced partnerships, so they can cope with situations that formerly baffled them.

Obviously you won't get far using advanced techniques with a retarded partner who plays by rote. But winning bridge is not played by rote. So this section of the book is only for you and your favorite partner who thinks before he plays and knows what he is about.

Each of you will learn why certain techniques succeed against first-class opposition and why others fail. Throughout we will assume you are playing against equally advanced players who will be tuned in to your bidding and can be counted on to use it to their own advantage. So you will learn how to get to optimum contracts without telling the other side too much. Nothing secretive and certainly not unethical—but a legitimate way to cloak your hand when you wish and reveal it fully to partner when *he* needs to know (but not until then).

Here, then, is a brief summary of the points we will cover in this advanced section:

1. A streamlined 15-to-17-point notrump for advanced players who get more out of their hands through superior dummy play.

2. A long hard look at the point-count scale: why the ace is undervalued; effect of honors in combination and as singletons and doubletons; the rare times it pays to open one notrump with a 5–4–2–2 or 6–3–2–2 shape.

3. Deceptive use of the Stayman two-club bid (no longer guaranteeing a 4-card major suit), to keep the other side in the dark.

4. Expanded use of responder's minor-suit rebid at the three level after Stayman to reach smoothly 4–3 major-suit games, minor-suit games and slams that depend on fit.

5. The new Stayman two-diamond convention in response to one notrump —to disclose the unstopped suit and find superior minor-suit games and slams.

6. A 12-to-14-point weak notrump, nonvulnerable—for greater preemption and competition, coupled with "nonforcing" Stayman to help scramble out of trouble; the raise to two notrump to ask for minors.

7. A nonvulnerable notrump overcall, based on a long escape suit in a weak hand, that puts the opponents off balance without giving up the classic notrump overcall.

8. The pros and cons of artificial bids and how to deal with them.

9. The little-understood means of reaching slams that depend upon fit; when and how to use Gerber and Blackwood; how to adjust your bidding to weak two-bids.

Ready for the expert league?

THE STREAMLINED NOTRUMP—

AND SOME OBSERVATIONS

ABOUT POINT COUNT

IN THE FAST-PACED world of bridge, it is the hidebound citizen who pays the upkeep. The winning bridge player is both progressive and realistic; he sets out to gather all the evidence about him, sifts it, and only then decides upon his course of action; he consciously tries to rid himself of preconceptions that adversely affect judgment.

That, dear reader, is our little preamble to asking a favor of you. But what we really want is for you to do yourself a favor. We want you to make an adjustment in the sacrosanct and classic requirements for an opening notrump. There! We've said it! Instead of the well-remembered 16-to-18-point range, we now ask you to adopt a 15-to-17-point range. (Don't panic: this simple adjustment does not affect the bidding superstructure and dictates no change in any other notrump bid—neither the notrump overcall nor opening bids of two and three notrump.)

This slight change will pay large dividends. In any event, the 16–18-point range is not some inviolate institution that has been handed down from generation to generation and withstood the tests of time—like monogamy. Older players will remember when the upper limit was 19 points. And before that— in the prepoint-count era—an opening notrump bid was based on "honor tricks." So we have ample precedent for asking you to change your thinking.

WHY 15 POINTS?

We have stressed earlier that the opening bid of one notrump is the most precise single bid in the lexicon of bridge. Therefore, we want to use this admirable tool on as many hands as possible. Unless you are an exceptional card holder, over the long pull you will hold more 15-point hands than 18-pointers. Ergo, when we lower the requirements to 15 points, we are able to open one-notrump more often. And that is just our goal, for it starts the auction off on a solid base.

WHY NOT GO LOWER?

Once we start to lower the floor for an opening notrump, why stop at 15 points? What about going down to 14 or 13, so we can open with a notrump on many more hands? When it is safe, we suggest just that. Nonvulnerable, we recommend a 12-to-14-point range, as you will see in Chapter 12. But for safety's sake 15 points is about the rock bottom for a vulnerable notrump. Below that you stand to lose more than you'll gain; it is almost child's play for the opponents to double you for penalties. Remember the notrump bid puts you at the outer limit of the one level; if it turns out to be the wrong spot, there is no running backward to rescue at the one level. If you bail yourself out into a suit, it has to be at the two level—and this is where some of the juiciest doubles are racked up. Safety first, say we; stick to a floor of 15 points when vulnerable.

AND WHY 17 POINTS?

There are several good reasons for adjusting the upper limit to 17 points. First, it is preferable to keep a constant spread between a maximum and minimum opening notrump. You will bid more accurately when you know your partner's strength down to the value of a queen. It is also easier to classify hands within a 3-point range; either you have a maximum, an average or a minimum; there are only those three possibilities. When we lower the floor of the notrump bid by 1 point, we have to drop the ceiling by the same amount—or else change our classification scheme.

Besides, how far can you go in changing bridge players' habits? We are all used to this 3-point range; if it were narrowed to 2 points, for example, we would have to make complicated adjustments throughout the rest of the bidding structure as compensation.

Another reason is that 18 points represents a powerful hand to a skillful player who gets more out of his cards. Such hands should be bid aggressively—opening one in a suit and jumping in notrump on the next round.

ADJUSTMENTS IN RESPONSES

Surprisingly, the 15-to-17-point notrump forces very few adjustments on the responder. He no longer invites game with a bare 8 points, for game prospects are too sketchy. But he still suggests game with a solid 8-pointer and insists upon game with 10 points.

If this sounds inconsistent, consider these two factors: advanced players have a better chance to make a game with 25 points—even against advanced opposition. Declarer retains the advantage of the blind opening lead; during the subsequent play, he knows his side's entire twenty-six cards, while each opponent has to dope out this information as the play proceeds. The higher the level of bridge, the more this advantage accrues to declarer.

Secondly, this is a different 25-point combination than the one we cautioned against earlier. In Chapter 2, we advised average players to steer clear of game when the points were divided 16-9. But when they are 15-10, there is more balance between the two hands, less of a communication problem; hence a better chance for a better player to bring home his game contract.

A FEW POINT-COUNT POINTERS

The acceptance of point count was a significant breakthrough in bridge bidding, for it translated elements of strength into a convenient common denominator. More than any other development in the last generation, point count sparked the new wave of bridge popularity.

But point count has its limitations. It is a handy measuring stick—nothing more, not a miracle drug, or a substitute for judgment.

The 4-3-2-1 point scale is easy to remember and calculate; paradoxically, that is its inherent weakness. It is both arbitrary and inaccurate, for it rejects fractional points which more accurately reflect the true values. Although various experiments have been tried, fractional points have not taken hold and it is too late in the day to change bridge players' habits. However, advanced players should be aware of the distortions within the accepted point-count scale.

THE ACE IS UNDERVALUED

The ace is really worth more than 4 points. At one time we recommended a valuation of 4½ points, but this count proved to be too complicated for players accustomed to a whole-number scale. So we have reluctantly gone along with the standard point scale, but we recommend adjustments for the advanced player to provide helpful guidelines in making close bidding decisions.

The ace acts like a fairy godmother over smaller honors, giving them protection and greater utility. Thus, we should mentally increase the value of A J, A Q or A K in the same suit. Whether you add ½ point, or a plus value or merely think more highly of the holding is a matter of temperament; the important thing is to recognize the promoted worth.

Let's examine a few holdings to see how they are worth more:

(1) A K x. The presence of the ace makes the king a sure trick and a sure stopper. In theory, this holding is worth no more than A x x opposite K x x, for it still produces two tricks and two stoppers. But when you hold A x x, partner might have his king in another suit where it is good for only one-half a trick. When you can see both top honors in your own hand, you do not have to speculate whether partner has second-round control of the suit.

(2) A Q x. The queen alone is worth only one-quarter of a trick. In combination with the ace it is worth more than half a trick. When the opening lead is in the suit, declarer's A Q becomes two sure tricks. If the suit is not opened, declarer has a simple finesse for two tricks. Compare this with A x x opposite Q x x. You still have an even chance of scoring the queen by leading up to it, but you will have to surrender the lead in the process. With A Q x, you merely take the finesse and keep the lead if it works.

(3) A J x. This holding is more difficult to evaluate. If both the king and queen are to your right, the holding produces two tricks, whereas A x x opposite J x x will not unless the opponents are injudicious or are caught in some kind of throw-in. Even a ten from partner does for A J x what spinach does for Popeye.

ADJUSTMENTS FOR ACES

Our recommendation is to add 1 point for a holding of an ace with a lower honor. If this seems extravagant, remember that the ace is undervalued in the accepted point-count scale to start with, and the lower honor certainly increases in value when sheltered by the ace. Put the two increments together and they are easily worth a point.

Likewise, a hand with all four aces is conservatively worth a full point increase. And a hand without any ace should have a point shaved from its count. A simple and logical way to remember this is to consider two aces as "par" for an opening one-notrump bid: then add ½ point for each extra ace and deduct ½ point for each ace below par. This scale produces the adjustments just suggested: +1 for four aces, −1 for no aces. Going further it adds ½ for three aces and deducts ½ for one ace. This approach is useful in deciding borderline bids.

"WORKING" HONORS

Honor cards in combination with each other are worth more than isolated honors. Since the ace is "top dog," it affords maximum promotion to the lower honor. But the same principle applies to lower honors. A holding of J x x, Q x x or even K x x has a somewhat indeterminate value. But Q J x, K J x and K Q x have more solid playing strength. Again it is impossible to assign a precise value to honors in combination; it is enough that you recognize that they are worth more.

SINGLETON AND DOUBLETON HONORS

If a bridge player could switch around his honor cards at will, he would always have combinations of honor cards heading up his long suits, because the top-card strength would help make winners of the spot cards. But we have to play the cards we are dealt and thus we have to contend with singleton and doubleton honors.

We do not deduct anything for a singleton ace. The ace is still the "top dog" that is underrated in the present scale.

But we do deduct a point for a king, queen or jack singleton; likewise we deduct 1 point from any doubleton honor lacking the ace: K Q, K J, Q J. These junior honors lose their mobility without a companion spot card. If a lower spot card were available, it could be shed when a higher honor is played. Without the spot card, the honor is denuded and may drop willy-nilly under an opponent's honor.

We could go one step further and deduct something for the doubletons Q x and J x. Certainly they are worth less than Q x x and J x x, but it is splitting hairs to decide how much. So this is where we draw the line.

RECAP OF POINT ADJUSTMENTS

. . . Add 1 point for A J, A Q, A K.

. . . Add $1/2$ point for each ace more than two.

. . . Deduct $1/2$ point for each ace less than two.

. . . Upgrade Q J x, K J x, K Q x—about $1/2$ point.

. . . Deduct 1 point for doubleton honors unaccompanied by a small card, i.e., K Q, Q J, K J, and for singleton honors, king, queen, jack.

AN EXERCISE IN HAND VALUATION

There is great leverage in honor combinations that form a tenace. Compare these two 17-point hands:

(1) ♠ A Q J ♡ 4 3 2 ◊ Q J 9 8 ♣ A Q J
(2) ♠ A K ♡ 8 7 6 2 ◊ K 5 4 3 ♣ A K 4

In (1) there are three possible tricks in each of the black suits, if the king is onside. Even if the king is wrong, each suit will produce two sure tricks. No power on earth can get more than two tricks out of either black suit in (2). Yet we are told to count each black suit in (2) at 7 points. Surely the black-suit holdings in (1) are worth more than 7 points.

The utility of honor combinations is reinforced by the presence of high spot cards. Examine the diamond holdings in these two hands and assume your partner (North) has only two small cards in the suit. With (1) you are sure of one diamond trick and have an even chance of netting two (by finding East with the ten and finessing against it twice). But with (2), you have only a 50–50 chance of making just *one* trick and none whatsoever of making two. Which holding would you rather have?

DON'T GO OVERBOARD

Most players tend to overlook favorable honor-card combinations; it is also tempting to err in the opposite direction. On (1), for example, it would be unrealistic to credit 1 extra point for each of the advantageous holdings in spades, diamonds and clubs. This is the same danger as figuring on too many distributional points.

There are *always* 40 high-card points in the deck and no more. If you count too many points for distribution or honor-card combinations, you may find yourself in game or slam with insufficient high cards. For example, if you give yourself 3 extra points on (1) ànd arrive at slam, those 3 "found" points will be offset by 3 high-card points in the opponent's hands; it might be in the form of a vital king that sets your slam.

HOW MANY POINTS?

We hesitate to assign precise values for any holding. It is enough to know which combinations are advantageous and which are not pulling their weight. Once a player can see this for himself—without a series of point-count adjustments—he is on the right track and can make his own judgment.

As a practical matter, we would open (2) above with one notrump under the 15-to-17-point scale, but would consider (1) too strong for an opening notrump. It is a bit excessive to credit (1) with an extra point for *each* of three favorable suit holdings. If pressed for a numerical valuation, we would allow an extra 1½ or 2 points and let it go at that.

IT ALL DEPENDS!

But in bridge very little is what it seems. Assume you decide to open both hands with one notrump and in each case hear a three-heart response from partner. Which hand do you like better now? Obviously (2). Why? Well, because of, first, better trump support; second, a doubleton that will produce an extra ruffing trick at suit play; third, better controls in the side suits.

Hand (1) is better for *developing* tricks, but (2) gets the nod for *controlling* suits—that is, for preventing the defenders from grabbing tricks off the top.

If North happens to hold:

♠ 8 7 5 2 ♡ A Q J 9 5 ◊ A 7 ♣ 6 2

he can breeze home to a heart slam with (2) as dummy; but opposite (1), he has a potential loser in each suit.

The moral of this tale is: *Re-evaluate.* Your work is not done just because you've totaled up your points and find you can open with one notrump. Partner's suit response may suddenly make your hand look a lot better—or worse.

UNBALANCED NOTRUMP OPENERS

What would you bit with this hand?

♠ A Q ♡ 9 7 6 4 ◊ A Q ♣ K J 7 6 3

Technically, the hand is too "unbalanced" for a notrump opener, yet this is the rare case where one notrump is the proper opener for a 5–4–2–2 shape. The two A Q doubletons make the difference. If you make any other opening bid, partner may declare at notrump. He won't enjoy an opening lead through one of your A Q doubletons. Therefore, foresight dictates that you bid notrump first. If either doubleton were weaker than A Q, one club would be the preferable bid.

Now try this one:

♠ A Q ♡ 8 5 2 ◊ A 10 ♣ K Q J 10 8 6.

Right you are: we're plumping for one notrump again—6-card suit and all. The future of this hand appears to be in notrump: against a spade lead you have eight tricks in your own hand, so why waste your time stalking an eleven-trick club game? Compare with the previous example: the extra club compensates for the diamond queen, so you don't need A Q in *both* doubletons.

BREAKING THE RULES

As you get to know more about bridge and understand the theory of bidding, you can break the rules more often.

Earlier we set Q x x x as the minimum "biddable" 4-card major opener could name after a Stayman inquiry. Better not shade *this*, for it is dangerous to play in a trump suit where the opponents have most of the high-card strength; when the trumps are banked, you'll surely be doubled and set badly. Ordinarily two or three high trump honors are insurance against these disastrous doubles. Then the opponents may not find the double, and even if they do, they won't be able to "draw your trumps." Take an extreme case:

NORTH: 8 6 4 2
SOUTH: 9 7 5 3

If you could be sure trumps would break 3–2, this is a playable suit. But if one opponent has four cards, he can draw your trumps and immediately set your contract of four spades. And all the time you might easily have nine running tricks in the other three suits.

In short, missing an ace, king and queen, we'll rest easier if they're outside the trump suit. But even this "rule" can be broken. At match points we'd respond to two clubs, Stayman, with any motheaten 4-card major. If we are doubled and go for 1100 once, for a bottom, it is offset by the time we make five spades for a top while the rest of the field is making only four notrump.

Throughout this book we try to set up guidelines rather than rigid rules. In many cases there is no "perfect" bid, only a choice between two actions, each with its own drawbacks. The art of good bidding is to choose the bid that has the lesser disadvantage—a choice between evils.

But in Part I, designed for average players, we couldn't explain all the whys and wherefores. We had to be arbitrary at times. For example, in Chapter 1, we stated that a major suit as good as K J x x x disqualifies a hand for an opening notrump bid. As we look back, that is too rigid a rule. What we really mean is that we'd rather open one in a major if the suit is playable opposite a small doubleton in partner's hand. And what is "playable"? Well, we'd say a suit that figures to hold the losses to two tricks. For example:

NORTH: 3 2
SOUTH: Q J 10 9 8

Q J 10 9 2 is good enough, maybe even Q J 10 8 2. But Q 9 5 4 3? No. By these standards K J x x x is not a "playable suit"—but you have to draw the line somewhere, and this is as good as any for the average player. But now that you understand the principle, you can set up your own guideline so that you will not open one notrump with a playable 5-card major suit.

There are 635 billion possible hands you can hold and a strictly limited vocabulary with which you can describe them. No bidding system can possibly give you the definitive bid for each possible hand. To steer your way through this maze requires judgment—not slavish adherence to set rules and point-count tables.

It is the same in the larger realm of life itself. Language is the *means* of communication—not the *substance*. Thoughts originate, not in the larynx, but in the brain.

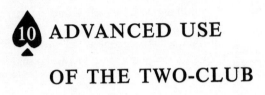

ADVANCED USE

OF THE TWO-CLUB

STAYMAN RESPONSE

No EXPERIENCED bridge player is so confident of his ability that he lets an opponent look at his hand during the auction. Yet a great many players seem to go out of their way to give the other side a similar advantage during the bidding. This comes about because they are using a straightforward system that contains no deceptive features to keep the opposition off balance. Earlier we observed that a successful system must have this maneuverability.

"STRAIGHT" STAYMAN

The difficulty of playing Stayman as we have already outlined it is that the two-club response to one notrump guarantees at least one 4-card major suit. It is all very well to make promises to partner, but there are no secret covenants in bridge. When you give partner your solemn word, you also make a guarantee to the opponents. Surely, no earthly good can result from making firm promises to the opponents.

THE BEST OF BOTH WORLDS

The responder's objective is clear enough; to find out about partner's major suits without revealing anything about his own. This can be accomplished, but it requires a basic realignment of thinking. The primary tenet that responder guarantees one 4-card major in responding two clubs must be discarded.

The opener continues to give accurate answers to the questions responder asks him, but he is no longer allowed to "correct" the contract to a major suit, under the assumption that partner has four cards in one of them. Under this new method, he is aware that responder may be setting up a smokescreen.

DISCIPLINE PAYS OFF

The new controlled rules preserve all the advantages of having the right tools to find major-suit fits; but the exciting new element is that you no longer have to give the show away to the opening leader. *That* is the over-riding incentive and that is where you reap unexpected rewards. If the man on lead is in a quandary, his wonder can make you a winner.

EXAMPLES

The bidding has been:

SOUTH	NORTH
1NT	2♣
2♠	3NT
?	

and you, South, hold:

(1) ♠A Q 6 4 ♡ K J 8 5 ◇ A 5 ♣ Q 6 2. *Pass.* Formerly you would have bid four hearts automatically, because partner's two-club bid guaranteed four cards in one of the majors. Since he didn't like spades, he must have hearts. Now that we have removed this guarantee, you must assume partner knows what he is doing. As we shall see, North could have investigated the heart situation by bidding three clubs or three diamonds at his second turn. Since he did not, it is now apparent to everyone at the table that he was kidding with his two-club bid and has no interest in the majors. But *you* are the only one who knows that there are four fair hearts resting in your hand; the auction has kept West honest and he might open a heart up to your strength —all because the bidding did not let the cat out of the bag. Even if nothing has been gained by the maneuver, neither has anything been lost.

Now take this auction:

SOUTH	NORTH
1NT	2♣
2♡	3NT

Under our new thinking, North may have either of the following hands:

(1) ♠ K J 6 5 ♡ A Q 9 ◇ 1 0 7 6 4 3 2 ♣ None
(2) ♠ 7 3 ♡ 6 4 ◇ A Q J 1 0 6 2 ♣ K 9 8

As the bidding develops, he does not have to reveal his spade holding, so · West has to choose his opening lead in the blind. West may suspect tomfoolery, but unless he has a marked lead, he will probably open a minor suit on the supposition that North has four spades. If North holds (2) above, this favorable opening lead may be just what is needed to bring home the contract. But North cannot bid a deceptive two clubs on (2) if his partner is allowed to take out three notrump into four hearts when he holds both majors.

The bidding has been:

SOUTH	NORTH
1NT	2♣
2♠	2NT
?	

and you, South, hold:

(1) ♠ K J 7 5 ♡ K 8 6 3 ◇ Q 9 ♣ A Q 4. *Pass!* This answer will probably stick in the craw of 98 percent of all bridge players, for they feel it is dirty pool to withhold the second major. Well, let's take a closer look. Is there game in the hand? No, for you have a minimum and partner has 9 points at most. Won't three hearts be a better contract? Perhaps, if partner has four hearts, but remember he is allowed to bid Stayman without any 4-card major. Now the crucial question: *Can you play in three hearts? No!* It is an absolute force to game. (Once you start with Stayman any bid at the three level in a suit that may not fit partner is forcing to game.) In short, you might make two notrump, but would be over your head in any game contract. So pass and hope for a profit.

SAFEGUARDS

Responder will not hit trouble with his partner when he adopts the new philosophy. There are always ways to solicit the information he wants and to obscure the bidding when that is his aim. On occasion, he will have to get to game "by way of Chicago" but it is worth it because it keeps the opening leader off balance.

THREE CLUBS OR THREE DIAMONDS
FOR EXPLORATION

In the first bidding sequence we used as illustration—

SOUTH	NORTH
1NT	2♣
2♠	3NT

—we said that South should pass, for North must know what he is about. The corollary to this is that North has another means of investigating the heart suit when he holds four hearts. This tool is a rebid of three clubs or three diamonds. The message is: "Tell me more about your hand, partner. As for mine, I'm strong enough to insist on game and may have slam interest; my hand is oriented to the minor suit I bid."

DON'T REHASH YESTERDAY'S NEWS

This does not mean that opener should repeat the message already given. Nothing is as stale as yesterday's newspaper. Usually, opener's response to two clubs has told the whole story about his holding in the majors. *Two hearts* says, "I have four hearts." *Two diamonds* states, "I do not have four cards in either major."

But *two spades* is an ambiguous answer, for it tells nothing about the heart situation. Therefore, in this auction:

SOUTH	NORTH
1NT	2♣
2♠	3♣ (or 3♢)

opener's first duty is to clarify the heart story. With four hearts, opener merely rebids three hearts. (There is no point to jumping to four hearts, as a game-forcing situation already exists.)

DESCRIBE THE IMPORTANT FEATURE

If opener does not have four hearts, he uses the available bidding space at the three level either to announce a fit with partner's minor or to express his preference for playing at three notrump, with a minimum.

HOW MUCH FIT?

From your opening notrump bid, partner will assume that you have 3-card support. Therefore a "fit" should mean something more—specifically, four cards. And not just any four cards—but something like Q J x x—qualifies as a good fit with partner.

SHOWING THE FIT

The direct way to show any fit is to raise the suit. But, in this instance, that takes us to the four level. It is more economical and constructive to bid a new suit in which you have top-card strength at the three level. By inference, this shows a fit with partner's suit. No other feature could have improved the hand you announced earlier with your one-notrump bid.

A few illustrations will clarify how this theory works in practice: The bidding has been:

SOUTH	NORTH
1NT	2♣
2♠	3♣
?	

and you, South, hold:

(1) ♠ K 7 6 4 ♡ Q 9 7 5 ◇ A K ♣ K 10 3. *Bid three hearts.* Your first duty is to show that you have four hearts as good as Q x x x. The heart bid is mandatory.

(2) ♠ K 7 6 4 ♡ Q 7 ◇ A K 6 ♣ K Q 10 3. *Bid three diamonds.* You do not hold four hearts, but have excellent club support. Therefore, choose the bid at the three level that best describes your hand. Partner might be most interested in knowing that you have top diamond strength.

(3) ♠ K 7 6 4 ♡ A J 7 ◇ A 6 4 ♣ Q J 10. *Bid three notrump.* Lacking a 4-card heart suit and a good club fit with partner, rebid in notrump to indicate that you have a minimum notrump and want to play the hand at three notrump. Partner will be able to deduce that your strength is evenly distributed.

(4) ♠ K 7 6 4 ♡ A J 7 ◇ A 6 ♣ Q J 10 4. *Bid three diamonds.* Your hand is no longer a 15-point minimum notrump, for the combination of a side doubleton and 4-card trump support usually produces an extra ruffing trick or two. You would prefer to have more in diamonds for your encouraging bid, but there is no satisfactory alternate bid: three notrump would denote a flat hand; three hearts or three spades would indicate length in the bid suit and four clubs puts you past three notrump. So by the process of elimination, three diamonds is our choice.

(5) ♠ K 7 6 4 3 ♡ A Q 7 ◇ K J 4 ♣ Q 3. *Bid three spades.* This tells partner, first, you do not have four hearts; and second, you have a 5-card spade suit. (Your previous bid told him you had four spades, so the rebid shows five.)

(6) ♠ A K J 6 ♡ K 6 ◇ Q 5 2 ♣ K J 8 3. *Bid four clubs.* You would like to rebid three spades to show the solid top spades and a good club fit. But three spades, in this sequence, shows a 5-card suit—see (5). You can't use the same bid to describe two different kinds of holdings. The red suits might prove your undoing at three notrump, so you choose a club raise, rather than a three-notrump rebid, to steer partner toward a club game. Besides, the club raise is the only direct way to show both a club fit and a maximum notrump. Ofttimes the simple, straightforward bid is the best of all.

AFTER TWO DIAMONDS OR TWO HEARTS

The same principles apply when opener's first rebid is two diamonds or two hearts, except that there is no longer any ambiguity about opener's heart holding. He has either announced four cards in the suit (by bidding two hearts) or denied such a holding (by bidding two diamonds). In the rare case when opener has *five* hearts, he will later rebid the suit to show the extra length, if possible.

ILLUSTRATIVE HANDS

The bidding has gone:

SOUTH	NORTH
1NT	2♣
2◇	3◇
?	

and you, South, hold:

(1) ♠ A K J ♡ K Q 6 ◇ K J 7 5 ♣ 8 7 2. *Bid three spades.* This confirms the diamond fit with a full value opening and locates the concentration of your side strength. Your previous two-diamond bid announced that you did not have four spades, so this bid cannot be misconstrued to show spade length.

(2) ♠ K 7 5 ♡ A Q 6 ◇ Q J 7 4 ♣ A 6 4. *Bid three hearts.* Again, bid the suit of massed strength when you have a fit with partner. This is as good a place as any to define "massed strength" or "concentration of strength." By these terms, we mean two of the top three honors: A K, A Q or K Q.

(3) ♠ K 9 5 ♡ K J 4 ◇ A Q 6 2 ♣ Q J 5. *Bid three notrump.* The hand isn't rich enough in high cards for you to be proud of it. By elimination, then, you settle for three notrump.

(4) ♠ K Q 7 ♡ A K 6 ◇ K Q 6 4 ♣ 8 6 4. *Bid three hearts.* Both major suits have massed strength, so you may as well show the stronger one. If both suits were equally strong, we would bid the lower ranking just to conserve bidding space. But don't trap yourself into bidding three notrump because of indecision about which suit to show. You must tell partner about your excellent diamond fit. There may be a diamond slam in the combined hands, and yet clubs could be your downfall at three notrump.

FINDING A 4–3 MAJOR FIT

Occasionally this refinement of the Stayman Convention will lead to an excellent 4–3 major-suit game:

The bidding:

SOUTH	NORTH
1NT	2♣
2◊	3♣
3♡	?

and you, North, hold:

(1) ♠ 8 5 3 ♡ Q J 10 2 ◊ J ♣ A Q 7 4 3. *Bid four hearts.* You know that South has only three hearts, but they are almost surely headed by the A K, since you hold the other heart honors. Moreover, South cannot have double stops in spades, hearts and diamonds, for he would have rebid three notrump with such a holding. So either spades or diamonds is his weak suit, a notrump game is unlikely, but a heart contract is promising, for the trump suit is likely to give you ultimate control of the suit the opponents attack. South's last bid confirms the club fit, so that suit is already set up to produce five tricks.

Now look at the hands in this example taken from actual play:

NORTH:	♠ 8 5 3	♡ Q J 10 2	◊ J	♣ A Q 7 4 3
SOUTH:	♠ Q J	♡ A K 4	◊ K 10 7 3	♣ K J 5 2

Unless the defense slips, three notrump doesn't have a prayer, for the opponents can take at least four spades and the ace of diamonds. But a heart game is odds-on. There are nine tricks on top in hearts and clubs and declarer has two good chances for a tenth: a spade ruff in the South hand or a successful diamond finesse.

Lucky, you say? Let's shift the South hand around a bit and observe the outcome:

(1)	NORTH:	♠ 8 5 3	♡ Q J 10 2	◊ J	♣ A Q 7 4 3
	SOUTH:	♠ A K 4	♡ K 7	◊ K 10 7 3	♣ K J 5 2

The bidding:

SOUTH	NORTH
1NT	2♣
2◊	3♣
3♠	3NT

South shows his spade strength and club fit. This reassures North on one of his weak suits. He can't be sure that three notrump will make, for the opponents may run the diamond suit. But North certainly doesn't want to play in four hearts when partner may have three small cards in the suit, or worse still, a doubleton. North reasons that either the opponents may not find the diamond suit or his singleton jack may be enough to stave off the onslaught until nine tricks can be run. As it happens, three notrump is ice cold.

(2)   NORTH: ♠ 8 5 3   ♡ Q J 10 2   ◇ J   ♣ A Q 7 4 3
       SOUTH: ♠ K 6 4   ♡ K 7   ◇ A K 10 3 ♣ K J 5 2

The bidding:

SOUTH	NORTH
1NT	2♣
2◇	3♣
3◇	3NT

This time the spade suit may be wide open, for North lacks an honor in the suit; but at least he has 3-card length. In any event, four hearts cannot be a good contract, so North gambles on three notrump. Note that North has never shown his heart suit, so the opponents have to guess at which major suit to open (their combined holding in each is seven cards). Three notrump is a splendid contract. If a spade is led, it takes a 5–2 spade break to defeat declarer; with any other lead, South knocks out the heart ace and scores nine tricks unless both the major-suit aces are unfavorably placed. Chances for bringing home the game are almost 75 percent.

(3)   NORTH: ♠ 8 5 3   ♡ Q J 10 2   ◇ J   ♣ A Q 7 4 3
       SOUTH: ♠ K Q 4   ♡ A K 7   ◇ Q 10 3   ♣ K 8 5 2

The bidding:

SOUTH	NORTH
1NT	2♣
2◇	3♣
3NT	Pass

South is just shy of a "good fit" with partner's clubs, so his three-notrump rebid is forced. North, of course, passes and three notrump is practically ironclad.

(4)   NORTH: ♠ 8 5 3   ♡ Q J 10 2   ◇ J   ♣ A Q 7 4 3
       SOUTH: ♠ K J 10   ♡ A K   ◇ Q 10 9 8   ♣ K J 5 2

The bidding:

SOUTH	NORTH
1NT	2♣
2◇	3♣
3NT	

South's book bid is three hearts to convey the club fit and the fine heart holding. However, South should go a step further in judging the situation. He has good stops in all suits, and his spade and diamond tenaces are more valuable if the lead comes up to them. His marked preference is for a three-notrump contract and that is the expert bid on this hand. Note that three notrump is child's play, but at five clubs, two spades and a diamond might be lost.

FINDING THE MINOR SUIT

The probing rebid of three in a minor opens the way for minor-suit games and slams:

NORTH: ♠ K 7 5 2   ♡ A 9   ♢ K J 6 4   ♣ 10 8 3
SOUTH: ♠ A Q 8   ♡ K Q 7 5   ♢ A Q 8 3   ♣ 9 7

SOUTH	NORTH
1NT	2♣ (a)
2♡	3♢ (b)
3♠ (c)	4♢ (d)
5♢ (e)	Pass (f)

(a) Looking for a 4–4 spade fit.

(b) Testing the diamond fit and asking for more information.

(c) "You found me: I have a good 4-card diamond fit, as well as spade strength and better than a minimum notrump. My previous bid proves that I am not showing a spade *suit*."

(d) Theoretically North could cue-bid the heart ace at this point, but he figures that a balanced hand of 11 points is not strong enough to offer this slam try. So he returns to the agreed trump suit at the cheapest level. (A game force still exists.)

(e) South has no ace to cue-bid so he has no choice but to bid game in the agreed suit. Even if North had cue-bid hearts on the previous round, South would have to subside, because he is staring at two baby clubs and his partner has given him no reassurance on this suit.

(f) Content.

This is very accurate and imaginative bidding and only a well-seasoned pair would find the diamond game while keeping out of slam. Perhaps you do not aspire to reach these difficult games. Still, don't dismiss the hand too quickly, for the superstructure of this auction will keep you out of unmakable notrump contracts. Take the same North hand and see what might happen if you decide to "cut out all that fancy stuff." Instead of bidding three diamonds at your second turn, you bid three notrump, OK? South has the same hand as shown above and a club is opened. Unless clubs are 4–4 or the suit blocks, down you go!

OPENER HAS THE SAME TOOL

The opener can get good mileage out of the same bid of three in a minor suit. Ordinarily his opportunity comes before responder has indicated whether he has a game-going hand; therefore, opener needs a maximum notrump in order to use the bid.

The bidding has gone:

SOUTH	NORTH
1NT	2♣
2◊	2♡
?	

and you, South, hold:

(1) ♠ K 5 ♡ K Q J ◊ A K 7 2 ♣ J 5 4 3. *Bid three diamonds.* This shows a good fit with partner's 5-card suit, a maximum notrump and top-card strength in diamonds. If responder is at all slam-minded, this news will be most welcome, whereas a four-heart bid uses up an extra bidding level without revealing the side strength.

(2) ♠ K Q 5 ♡ K Q 6 ◊ A 9 7 2 ♣ K 4 3. *Bid two spades.* Here is one of the rare cases where opener bids a *major* suit to show a suit fit and top-card strength. South's previous bid denied spade length, so he can show the suit now to tell about his top-card strength. Of course, the bid also indicates a fit with partner's suit and a maximum notrump. Again, it may pave the way for a slam.

GIVING RESPONDER ANOTHER CHANCE

Try this one. The bidding has gone:

SOUTH	NORTH
1NT	2♣
2♠	2NT
?	

and you, South, hold:

(1) ♠ K J 6 4 ♡ A Q 7 ◊ K Q 5 ♣ Q 8 5. *Bid three clubs or three diamonds.* Most players would bid three notrump without a second thought. But what if North holds hand (7), cited on page 36? Four hearts is odds-on, but three notrump bites the dust if West leads a diamond from A J x x and his partner has one of the black aces and pushes another diamond through the South hand.

How to get to four hearts? South doesn't need to be clairvoyant, only imaginative. Recognizing the possibility that North *might* have five hearts, he bids three of either minor. North now has room to show his hearts, and South raises to four.

(2) ♠ K J 6 4 ♡ A Q 7 4 ◇ K Q ♣ Q 8 5. *Bid three hearts,* not three of a minor. Since you have four hearts, bid them directly, rather than ask partner about his heart holding. If he has four hearts, he'll raise you to game. If not, he'll return to notrump. But can't he pass? No, because after Stayman, a bid of any *new* suit at the three level is forcing to game. You have to trust your partner to understand the implications. The alternative is to jump to four hearts—a bad bid with a good partner; remember that partner does not guarantee a 4-card major by his two-club bid; you won't relish playing four hearts with something like a 4-2 fit.

This is pretty high-level stuff and you may never run into some of the situations illustrated by the sample hands. The exact bidding sequences are, in themselves, unimportant, for we are not trying to teach you to bid specific hands. We *are* trying to lead you into a new way of thinking—a way of soliciting needed information about partner's hand to guide you in placing the final contract. This is a key foundation in the structure of creative bidding.

⑪ TWO DIAMONDS

FOR MINORS

DR. STAYMAN'S Spa for Tired Notrumps has done a booming business in the last decade, treating thousands of bridge players for third-degree burns, i.e., burned at three notrump when they should have been at four of a major. But until the ill was recognized, we couldn't prescribe the cure.

ONLY A MINOR ILL?

Now we set our sights on a new malady—being scalded at three notrump when eleven tricks at a minor suit are there for the taking. Most sufferers don't even know they have the disease and airily explain away such tragedies: "There was no way we could get to five clubs," or "I'd rather play for game at nine tricks than eleven."

Neither argument holds much weight. There is nothing in the bridge laws that prohibits a minor-suit game contract just because the opening bid happens to be one notrump. And no one in his right mind will argue that it is prudent to play for nine tricks at notrump with one suit wide open when there is a fighting chance to make eleven tricks at a minor suit.

Even the most experienced pairs find themselves at three notrump with an unguarded suit. Sometimes these contracts will make—when the opponents do not open that suit. However, no resourceful player wants to depend on a lucky suit lie or an opponent's slip when he can reach a superior contract that does not depend upon such good fortune.

IT HAPPENS ALL THE TIME

Enough theory. Try this hand with your favorite partner:

NORTH: ♠ K 10 5 ♡ K 6 4 ◊ A J 10 7 5 3 ♣ 8
SOUTH: ♠ A Q J ♡ Q J 7 ◊ Q 9 6 2 ♣ A 6 2

Unless you have remarkable partnership rapport, you'll probably arrive at three notrump. A club is led; declarer holds up for two rounds, finesses successfully for the diamond king and wraps up ten tricks. Nothing unusual about that, is there? But what if the diamond king were offside? You'd go down at three notrump—and there is a 50–50 chance that the diamond finesse will lose. Sure, you want to be in game with a 50–50 play for it. But you have the same 50–50 chance to make a *slam* in diamonds. Wouldn't you rather get the slam bonus for the same price of admission? This chapter will show you how to get to slam on such hands.

Here is an even stronger case: these are the same two hands except that North's ace has been switched to the heart suit:

NORTH: ♠ K 10 5 ♡ A K 6 ◊ J 10 7 5 4 3 ♣ 8
SOUTH: ♠ A Q J ♡ Q J 7 ◊ Q 9 6 2 ♣ A 6 2

Almost all partnerships will land at three notrump, using standard bidding methods. Again a club is lead, but this time there is no play for the contract. Yet, five diamonds is ice cold!

It is surprising how often this kind of thing pops up. A bit of diagnosis and some strong new medicine are definitely needed.

THE CARE AND FEEDING
OF UNBALANCED HANDS

Too many players get a notrump fixation after hearing an opening notrump bid across the table; they have the devil's own time bailing out into a superior minor-suit contract.

The most vexing case is when responder holds a worthless doubleton. This can sink a three-notrump contract, but it may also prove your undoing at five of a minor. If *both* partners hold doubletons in the same suit—and no stopper—the notrump contract is doomed. But five of a minor is no bed of roses either; unless the rest of the hand is absolutely solid or fits like a glove, the contract will fail.

In short, there is no sure solution to the symptom of the worthless double-ton. Responder has to be clairvoyant to know when to go for nine tricks at notrump and when to shoot for the eleven-trick minor-suit game. Our sug-gestion is to stick with the old-fashioned idea and gamble it out with an im-mediate bid of three notrump, staking your hopes on a favorable opening lead or fit. Notrump, after all, is the shortest way home; if you are set and later find five of a minor was on, you needn't cry your eyes out. It is not the worst tragedy known to mankind.

THE SINGLETON SYMPTOM

However, when responder holds a singleton, his hand screams out for ex-ploration. Unless opener is well-heeled in the suit, notrump will prove a rocky road. If partner holds less than four cards in the suit, the opponents have at least nine cards between them and it is very likely that they will open that suit. Ironically, it is just this combination of a singleton opposite weak-ness that makes five of a minor—or even slam in a minor—a heavy favorite. At a suit contract, a singleton in a side suit gives second-round control, and when the singleton is opposite small cards in partner's hand, there are no wasted honors and no duplication of values. Therefore the rest of the honor cards will be working at full capacity, and the hand should play well.

Conversely, if responder's singleton is opposite a double honor in partner's hand, it is very likely that declarer can hold off the run of the suit long enough to take nine tricks, and yet two honors opposite a singleton would be a clear duplication of values at a suit contract—a condition that would often doom the contract.

For these reasons, we have long felt a new approach was needed for game-going responding hands that include a singleton and length in the minors.

A CASE IN POINT

You, North, hold ♠ 6 ♡ K 5 3 ◊ K Q 9 6 ♣ A J 8 6 3 and the bid-ding has been:

SOUTH	NORTH
1NT	?

What do you bid?

Most players bid three notrump without a second thought, as if there were no other possible bid. Others try to muddy up the waters a bit by bidding two clubs, Stayman, en route to three notrump. Either way, three notrump may be an admirable contract, as, for example:

NORTH: ♠ 6   ♡ K 5 3   ◇ K Q 9 6   ♣ A J 8 6 3
SOUTH: ♠ K Q 4 ♡ A J 10 ◇ A J 7 5   ♣ 7 4 2

But three notrump could just as easily be a distinctly inferior contract if South holds something like:

NORTH: ♠ 6   ♡ K 5 3   ◇ K Q 9 6   ♣ A J 8 6 3
SOUTH: ♠ 7 4 2 ♡ A J 10 ◇ A J 7 5   ♣ K Q 4

There is no play for three notrump after a spade lead, and yet a slam in diamonds is a cinch.

STANDARD BIDDING FAILS

Under present bidding methods, North has no way of determining which of these two possible hands partner holds. The best he can do is to play the percentages, which clearly call for a bid of three notrump, because it requires two tricks less than a minor-suit game; furthermore, the odds are at least 3 to 1 against South's having a worthless holding in any one suit, since partner would not open one notrump with two unstopped suits.

Note how this hand bears out our earlier observation: when responder's singleton faces a worthless suit holding, the hand is ill suited for notrump play but ideal for suit play. When the singleton is opposite an honor holding, the suit is good enough at notrump but it represents duplication of values at suit play.

It does not occur to most players that the North hand above requires exploratory treatment. Often partner has just enough in the weak suit to bring home three notrump, and the few times three notrump fails are charged up to bad luck. But a thoughtful player does not leave to luck that which can be handled by skill. The two-diamond convention described below solves the dilemma for the experienced player. However, since it is a problem that many players do not even recognize, and since it covers situations that arise less frequently than the 4–4 major-suit fit, this convention will probably never have the wide acceptance of the two-club convention, though it is just as workable.

THE DECISIVE ADVANTAGE

Happily, the same convention that explores for minor-suit games also leads to many makable *slams:* anytime you are willing to commit for eleven tricks, just a shade more strength in the combined hands or a slightly better than usual fit can produce that extra trick for the slam. These slams can be bid.

TWO DIAMONDS IS THE TOOL

In the first part of this book, the two-diamond response to a one-notrump opening was defined as a weak bid, indicating a diamond suit and lack of game interest. Responder expects to be passed to play at two diamonds.

We are now going to give that response a more important role. Therefore, responder cannot take out to two diamonds and play at that spot. But this works no great hardship: responder has the option of stretching a bit to bid three diamonds or passing to one notrump. You can *create* hands that are set at one notrump and would make *exactly* eight tricks at diamonds, but they seldom crop up at the table; more often than not, aggressive opponents won't permit you to play at this low level. Even such occasional losses are more than offset by the minor-suit games and slams that are reached via the two-diamond convention. In short, more is going for you when you use two diamonds the modern way.

THE NEW MEANING

A two-diamond response to one notrump now becomes an artificial bid, forcing to game. It asks partner to describe his major-suit *stoppers* first and sets the stage to inquire about other features of opener's hand in later rounds, if responder wants a fuller picture. Responder uses the convention when he has a singleton or void and thus he can tell when his shortness is opposite an unstopped suit in partner's hand and can steer the contract to game or slam in a minor suit.

REQUIREMENTS FOR
THE TWO-DIAMOND RESPONSE

The two-diamond response promises four things to partner:

. . . At least 11 points in high cards.
. . . A singleton or void.
. . . At least five cards in one minor, and perhaps a minor two suiter.
. . . No interest in partner's major-suit length.

There is nothing arbitrary about these promises. Each is most logical. As to point count, responder must allow for the fact that the contract may play at five of a minor opposite a minimum notrump. Setting the lower limit at 11 points assures the partnership of a total of 26 high-card points, which should give them a good play for eleven tricks provided there is little duplication in the short suit.

A singleton in responder's hand is the clearest warning that a notrump contract may be hazardous. There is less reason to shy away from notrump holding a doubleton in the weakest suit, as pointed out earlier. Furthermore, a doubleton gives only third-round control in a suit; if the opponents take two quick tricks there, declarer has no margin for error in the rest of the play at five of a minor suit.

As to shape, there would be no reason for responder to suggest an eleven-trick minor-suit contract with a 4-card minor or 4-4 in the minors. His hand would then be either 4-4-3-2—which is balanced and suitable for notrump—or 4-4-4-1—an ideal shape for the Stayman two-club bid to investigate major-suit possibilities first. Remember, after starting with two clubs, responder can rebid three clubs or three diamonds at his next turn to show interest in a minor.

OPENER REPLIES

Over two diamonds, the opener has three bids with which to describe his major-suit stoppers:

Two notrump—"I have stoppers in both major suits."

Two spades—"I have a spade stopper, but no good heart stopper."

Two hearts—"I have a heart stopper, but no good spade stopper."

THE UNDERLYING THEORY

It is significant that the opener's first rebid concerns itself with stoppers. For the sake of simplicity, we have dealt with the two-diamond convention as aiming at a minor-suit fit. This really puts the cart before the horse. The basic purpose of the convention is to determine whether there is a flaw in the combined hands for notrump play in the form of a weakly guarded suit. It is only when a flaw is found that responder guides the auction away from notrump and toward game or slam in a minor.

When *either* partner can see that no flaw exists for notrump play, it is his duty to place the contract immediately at three notrump. There is no point in exchanging further information, because the opponents are listening while you chat.

If *responder* fails to bid three notrump at his second turn, obviously he wants to hear about a feature of opener's hand that is not yet disclosed. In general, it is this feature that will determine whether the hand will play at three notrump or at a minor-suit game or slam. We have already noted that the margin between eleven and twelve tricks at a minor suit is so slim that a careful exchange of information at a low level can make all the difference in making the right decision.

WHEN RESPONDER IS SHORT
IN A MAJOR SUIT

Responder's void or singleton may be in a major or minor suit. Let's take the major suit first. If opener has bid two notrump or the major suit in which responder is short, then responder merely rebids three notrump. He has been assured that the weak spot in his hand has adequate compensation in partner's so he will not avoid the natural nine-trick notrump game; of course, if responder has substantial extra values—enough to compensate for the announced duplication—he will make a slam try in any event.

But the convention earns its keep when opener's major-suit rebid is not in responder's short suit. Now responder knows the combined hands have a flaw for notrump. Therefore he bids three of his longer minor suit, which starts the partnership on the way to a minor-suit game or slam. (If his minors are equal in length, he bids them in natural order—the higher-ranking first.) Yet the bidding is still at the three level, and there is ample room for further exchange.

EXAMPLES

The bidding has been:

SOUTH	NORTH
1NT	2◇
2♠	?

and you, North, hold:

(1) ♠ 8 ♡ 9 7 3 ◇ A K Q 9 7 2 ♣ K 10 4. *Bid three notrump.* Since South has promised a spade stopper, your fears on that score are allayed. Furthermore, his spade strength will probably be wasted at a diamond contract. You have six running diamond tricks for a notrump contract, so that is your spot. Bid it directly without telling the opponents any more about your hand. Shouldn't you be worried about hearts? Not with three cards in the suit. The defenders can have, at most, eight hearts between them, and if they can run the suit, then you'd probably have no play at five diamonds either.

(2) ♠ 9 7 3 ♡ 8 ◇ A K Q 9 7 2 ♣ K 10 4. *Bid three diamonds.* Partner has denied a stopper in your singleton suit, so notrump is a madman's contract. Diamonds will be your best friend, and now it is just a matter of deciding whether to play for eleven or twelve tricks.

(3) ♠ 9 6 5 ♡ A Q 2 ◇ K Q 10 8 4 3 ♣ 6. *Bid three notrump.* South must have a good stopper opposite your singleton club, for he has already confessed lack of a good heart stopper. It is

inconceivable that he would open with a notrump with *two* questionable stoppers. (Even if South's rebid had been two hearts, we would recommend the same three-notrump call; you know the spades are the weak link, but they are just as fragile at a diamond contract as at notrump; all things considered, you have a better chance playing for nine tricks.)

WHEN RESPONDER IS SHORT IN A MINOR SUIT

Opener's two-notrump rebid discusses only *major*-suit stoppers. This does not resolve responder's problem when the latter's singleton or void is in a *minor* suit; at this stage he cannot determine whether the combined hands contain a flaw for notrump. Therefore responder continues the probing with a bid of three in his minor:

SOUTH	NORTH
1NT	2◇
2NT	3♣

South is now alerted to the probability that North has shortness in the other minor, diamonds. (If North were short in a major, the two-notrump bid would have allayed his fears and North would have bid three notrump at his second turn.) Hence South will not bid three notrump unless he has a good diamond stopper—a minimum of Q 10 x, as we play it. Lacking such a diamond stopper, South makes the most descriptive bid he can.

OPENER REVIEWS THE SITUATION

Opener's first response to the two-diamond inquiry is cut-and-dried, but his second demands thoughtful analysis and a restudy. In effect, his partner is asking two questions: (1) "Is notrump the right spot for us?" and (2) "If not, can you help me in deciding between game and slam in a minor suit?"

Opener has a number of factors to consider before expressing his view. At this juncture, he has a good idea of which is his partner's long minor suit and where his singleton (or void) is. And he re-evaluates his hand with that knowledge.

His reasoning should go something like this:

"1. *How do I support partner's suit?* If I have two of the top three honors and at least 3-card support, I want to encourage him. But I must also remember that this kind of support gives us a running suit for notrump. If I have the other extreme—a worthless doubleton—I want to discourage partner from getting up too high, for I cannot fill out his suit, and some of my honors in the other three suits are bound to be wasted. In this case, I'll try to play at three notrump.

"2. *How do I fit his singleton?* If I have three worthless cards, it means that all my other cards are just where he needs them. Likewise if I have A x x, there is no waste, for my ace eliminates his loser. But if I have K J x or Q J x, these are wasted in suit play and there will be a hole someplace else in the hand. In this case, I want to get to three notrump if possible.

"3. *How well do I control the other two suits?* Now that I have a good idea of partner's long minor and his short suit, do I have the top cards—the aces and kings—to prevent quick losers in those other two suits? If not, I want to discourage slam, and even eleven tricks may be too high, so again I'll push for three notrump."

In general, possession of aces should incline you toward a minor-suit game, while tenaces like K J x should persuade you to try notrump. Aces insure against the quick loss of tricks off the top. They are ideal for controlling a short suit in a trump contract. Yet at notrump they provide only a single stopper. A holding like Q J 10 9, on the other hand, is a sure double stopper at notrump, but won't prevent the opponents from taking the first two tricks off the top at suit play.

EXAMPLES

We will take several possible hands opener might have on this auction and in each case we will think them through to decide the most descriptive bid:

SOUTH	NORTH
1NT	2◇
2♡	3♣
?	

(1) ♠ J 8 7 ♡ A Q 10 ◇ A Q 9 ♣ K J 4 2. *Bid three hearts.* Three notrump is out because you don't have a spade stopper and partner's rebid confirmed that is his weak spot. You are on the way to a club game. On the way you should cue-bid your heart ace; if you get the chance you should also cue-bid the diamond ace to investigate slam possibilities. Each of these cue-bids implies good-looking clubs, for you wouldn't have opened a notrump if you were weak in both black suits.

(2) ♠ 9 6 2 ♡ K Q 8 ◇ K Q 10 ♣ A K 8 4. *Bid five clubs.* You have no red ace to cue-bid, yet you like the hand, for you have a maximum notrump, no wasted spade values and an excellent club fit. The jump in the agreed suit admirably describes the hand. Partner will know you have the club ace, since you have already denied a high spade honor and a red ace; you would hardly wax enthusiastic with an aceless wonder.

(3) ♠ 10 6 2 ♡ K Q 8 ◇ K Q 7 3 ♣ K Q J. *Bid four clubs.* Again, you have no red ace to show, but this time you have a minimum notrump. Since you can't pass or bid three notrump, four clubs is the

only call left. It is the weakest bid South can make since he must keep going.

(4) ♠ J 9 7 4 ♡ K Q 6 ◇ A 9 3 ♣ K Q 10. *Bid three notrump.* This shows a belated and partial spade stopper. By this time you should be disenchanted with your hand: it contains only one ace (two is par for an opening notrump), lacks four trumps or a side doubleton that might be useful for suit play.

RESPONDER'S MISSION

The two-diamond inquiry begins a dialogue. It is not simply an *interrogation* of opener, but rather an intelligent discussion with a clear purpose in mind. Responder has the obligation of cutting off loose talk and stopping at three notrump if he discovers that opener has an adequate stopper for his short suit. However, until that point he has to keep the conversation alive. Generally he will bid his longer minor suit at his second turn.

But that is not an automatic response by any means, for responder has the obligation of giving as well as receiving information. However, he may choose to conceal his long minor suit if the hand seems headed for notrump. Instead of painting a precise picture for the opponents, he will leave them a guess concerning his minor-suit holding.

Here are two possible auctions:

	SOUTH	NORTH
(1)	1NT	2◇
	2♡	2♠
(2)	1NT	2◇
	2♠	2NT

In both cases North is showing a probable stopper—or at least 3-card length—in the major suit opener did *not* bid. Further, he states that opener's unstopped major is not the "worry" suit—where he holds a singleton or void. Thereby North asks partner to unfold his story on minor-suit stoppers.

There is a subtle difference in the first auction, for North could bid two notrump to show a spade stopper; the fact that he bids two spades emphasizes that he has good spade strength—possibly a double stopper.

Note that responder does not jump to three notrump to close the bidding, but conserves a round of bidding by his two-notrump call. (The two-diamond bid established a game-forcing situation, so there is no risk opener will pass.)

Why does responder go to all this trouble to reassure his partner about his stopper in the weak major? He must have something else on his mind; he must be worried about the minors; his singleton or void is in a minor suit and he cannot proceed to three notrump until he knows partner has that minor adequately stopped. Thus either sequence asks opener, "How do we stand on the minors?"

THE FLAVOR OF THE AUCTION

Once you get the feeling of the thing, a number of thoughtful bidding dialogues are possible. Here's one:

NORTH: ♠ K 6 4 ♡ K 10 5 ◇ 8   ♣ A J 10 7 5 3
SOUTH: ♠ A Q 7 ♡ Q 6 ◇ K J 10 2 ♣ K 9 4 2

SOUTH	NORTH
1NT	2◇
2♠ (a)	2NT (b)
3NT (c)	

(a) Indicates a good spade stopper, but no good heart stopper.
(b) Announcing at least three hearts and probably a stopper and locating his singleton in a minor suit.
(c) Opener has a minimum and no reason to emphasize either minor suit, so he makes the natural rebid of three notrump. This promises stoppers in both minors.

Now with a different hand for opener:

NORTH: ♠ K 6 4 ♡ K 10 5 ◇ 8   ♣ A J 10 7 5 3
SOUTH: ♠ A Q 7 ♡ Q 6 ◇ A 7 6 2 ♣ K Q 6 2

SOUTH	NORTH
1NT	2◇
2♠	2NT
3♣ (a)	3♠ (b)
4◇ (c)	6♣ (d)

The first four bids are the same, but this time the partnership is warned away from notrump:

(a) With a maximum notrump (17 points) and exceptional strength in the minors, South is right in making an encouraging rebid. Three clubs is a well-chosen move: South prefers a club contract and hopes that North's longer suit is clubs, for then South's diamond ace will cover North's declared singleton. Furthermore, if South had 4-card suits headed by two high honors in both minor suits, he should still bid the lower-ranking one; this gives North the chance to bid three diamonds, if that is his suit, and conserves bidding room.

(b) The three-spade bid paints a near-perfect picture of the North hand. It confirms that clubs are indeed the longer minor (if North had a long diamond suit, he would rebid three diamonds, or possibly three notrump, instead). Therefore he has a singleton diamond. He has previously announced a heart stopper and how he shows a high spade honor. Adding it all up, North in three bids has told partner he has: probably 3-3-1-6 distribution,* high honors in both spades and hearts, a good club suit and at least 11 points.

(c) South dutifully cue-bids the diamond ace, for he is willing to go places.

(d) This is all North needs to bid the slam. If he is the suspicious sort, he could first check for aces via a Blackwood four-notrump bid, but this is somewhat like a sculptor using a sledgehammer after he has worked delicately with a fine chisel. South has already cue-bid the diamond ace, and his sturdy spade stopper must include the ace (North himself is looking at the king): besides South could scarcely bid as aggressively as this without two aces.

Now put yourself in South's shoes after this auction:

SOUTH	NORTH
1NT	2♦
2NT	3♣

You, South, hold:

♠ A 6 4 ♡ K 10 7 ◇ K Q 7 5 ♣ A 9 8.

What do you bid? Let's analyze this hand according to the three criteria set forth earlier:

1. *Support for partner's club suit*: Adequate, but nothing to rave about. Four-card length or a second honor *would* be something.

2. *Holding opposite partner's singleton (probably in diamonds):* You have a good double stopper for notrump, but these may be 5 wasted points for suit play.

3. *Holding in the side suits*: Fine, nothing below a king.

Put it all together and the hand calls out for notrump, not suit play. Hence, you bid *three notrump*.

In this example, you, as South, gave your opinion that three notrump is the best spot. But this is not binding upon partner. Let's take the same hand one step further in the auction to see what happens when partner bids over three notrump:

---

* North's shape could be 3-2-1-7, 2-2-1-8, 3-3-0-7 or a number of other freak distributions, but he cannot be any more balanced than 3-3-1-6 on this bidding. Let's work backward to see why this holds true: North must have a singleton—in this case in diamonds; he has no "interest in partner's major-suit length," hence he cannot have as many as four cards in either major; he has, therefore, at most three cards in each major and a singleton diamond, and the rest of his hand must be in clubs—a 6-card suit at the least.

SOUTH	NORTH
1NT	2♦
2NT	3♣
3NT	4♦
?	

At first, North's bidding seems inconsistent. Your two-notrump bid reassured him that both major suits were stopped for notrump play. Therefore his bid of three clubs seems to indicate that he is short in diamonds and is worried about that suit for notrump. Dutifully, you calmed his fears on that score, bidding three notrump to show a diamond stopper also. And still he wouldn't stay put. What does it all mean?

Just that he is not short in diamonds at all. North must have at least a 4-card suit for his diamond bid, and, since he bid clubs first, at least five clubs. Hence he is short in one of the major suits. Why then wouldn't he be content to play at three notrump? Apparently he is looking for bigger game; therefore we conclude that he has more than 11 points or a very unbalanced hand —which amounts to the same thing.

Now that you know more about North's hand, how does yours fit with his? Well, you have an ideal fit in diamonds, and your club ace solidifies that suit. There is probably no club loser, or, at worst, a finesse in the suit. All of a sudden, your hand looks a lot better and you want to encourage partner. You could bid five diamonds, but that would only indicate a good 4-card diamond holding and would leave him in the dark about your club help and spade ace. No, you want to give him more encouragement than that. The master bid is four spades, to show the spade ace, and, by inference, a good diamond fit. (Don't "cue-bid" the club ace, for a five-club bid would be interpreted as a preference for clubs over diamonds.)

It is time to look at both hands together:

NORTH: ♠ 9 ♡ Q 5 ♦ A J 8 4 ♣ K Q 10 7 4 3
SOUTH: ♠ A 6 4 ♡ K 10 7 ♦ K Q 7 5 ♣ A 9 8

After South's four-spade bid, a small slam should be reached; how is largely a matter of style. North could bid six diamonds directly, relying on your implied 4-card diamond fit; he could try six clubs, to show the extra club length, allowing you to choose between the minor suits.

Here are a few more thoughtful auctions. The bidding has gone:

SOUTH	NORTH
1NT	2♦
2♡	2NT
?	

and you, South, hold:

(1) ♠ J 8 6 ♡ A Q 6 ◇ K J 5 ♣ K Q 10 6. *Bid three notrump.* This is a good descriptive call. You have double stoppers in both minor suits. Whichever is partner's singleton, it is adequately covered for notrump play. But this strength is likely to be a waste for minor-suit play.

(2) ♠ J 8 6 ♡ A K 6 ◇ A 9 5 2 ♣ K Q 8. *Bid three clubs.* This does *not* show the ace of clubs, because you cannot cue-bid an ace until you know partner's suit. Perhaps it strikes you odd to bid a 3-card minor suit lacking the ace when you could bid a 4-card minor suit headed by the ace. This is just one illustration of the rhythm created by the two-diamond inquiry. Partner's bidding indicates a singleton or void in one of the minor suits. If it is in diamonds and he has a long club suit, you want to encourage him all you can, and nothing will do that more than a club bid at this point. He already knows you do not have a spade stopper and won't proceed to a minor-suit slam—or perhaps even game—unless he has that department sewn up. But the rest of your hand could hardly be better for him: your ace of diamonds covers his probable singleton; you have the two top hearts and two of the top three clubs in support of his suit. A three-club bid also caters to the times he holds a diamond suit, because he now has room to bid it; let's say the bidding progresses:

SOUTH	NORTH
1NT	2◇
2♡	2NT
3♣	3◇

Now you'll be happy to settle for *three notrump.* Your K Q 8 of clubs opposite his singleton is no great shakes for a diamond contract; he has already told you he has the spades stopped; there is no flaw for notrump play but a distinct flaw in clubs for a diamond contract.

This hand illustrates the importance of an ace opposite partner's singleton.

RESPONDER CHANGES COURSE

Very little is routine in these sequences. Responder may have to ponder his decision carefully, even at his third turn. Take the situation from page 118 where South held ♠ J 9 7 4 ♡ K Q 6 ◇ A 9 3 ♣ K Q 10 and the bidding went:

SOUTH	NORTH
1NT	2◇
2♡	3♣
3NT	

What do you do, as North, with each of these hands?

(1) ♠ Q ♡ A J 7 ◇ 10 6 4 ♣ A J 9 7 4 3. *Pass.* The spade queen should bolster partner's partial stopper sufficiently to bring home the notrump game. As the cards lie, three notrump is cold, while five clubs offers only a remote play.

(2) ♠ None ♡ A J 7 ◇ J 8 6 4 ♣ A J 9 7 4 3. *Bid four clubs.* You can't stand notrump with a void opposite a secondary stopper. Be a good soldier and march along to your likely club game (ice-cold, as it happens, with partner's actual hand).

A void is not sufficient reason for responder to run from a notrump contract. It all depends on what opener has promised in the suit:

SOUTH	NORTH
1NT	2◇
2♡	?

You, North, hold:

(1) ♠ Q 8 6 ♡ None ◇ A K Q 8 5 3 ♣ J 9 4 2. *Bid three notrump.* Don't tell the opponents any more about your hand. You are not happy about the overlap in heart control and partner's lack of a spade stopper (oh, if it could have been the other way around!). But what can you do? You are off at least two spade tricks at any contract, so you had better play for nine tricks, not for eleven.

WITH A LONG MAJOR SUIT

Responder does not need the two-diamond convention when he holds a long major suit and a side singleton. He can effectively show extra values in one of two ways: (1) an immediate jump to three of the major, planning to rebid it over three notrump; this indicates some slam interest, for otherwise responder would have immediately jumped to four of his major; or (2) a Stayman two-club bid, persisting to game in his major.

WITH A 4-CARD MAJOR

Nor will responder use the two-diamond convention when he holds a 4-card major suit. Instead he bids two clubs, Stayman, to explore for the major-suit fit. If the fit does not materialize, he can rebid three of his longer minor and investigate the minor-suit possiblities. This sequence does not pinpoint the strength and distribution as accurately as the two-diamond convention, but there are no panaceas in bridge.

WITH A MAJOR-MINOR TWO SUITER

However, when responder holds a good 5-card major and a side minor suit, an advanced use of the two-diamond convention pays handsome dividends. Responder knows his partner has at least a doubleton in support of his major, so it is far more useful to learn about his high cards, rather than about his major-suit length. As the following hands illustrate, the two-diamond convention is superb for locating high cards. Therefore for maximum use of the convention we drop the requirement that responder have five cards in one minor suit:

(1)
NORTH:	♠ A Q 10 8 6 3	♡ Q J	◇ K J 7 5	♣ 4
SOUTH:	♠ K 7 2	♡ 9 6 3	◇ A Q 8 6	♣ A Q J

SOUTH	NORTH
1NT	2◇
2♠	4♠ (a)
Pass (b)	

(a) The two-spade bid told North that there are two heart losers in the hand, so he gives up on slam and settles for the spade game.

(b) South passes without a qualm, for North must want to play in four spades; otherwise he would have bid more gradually (the two-diamond bid creates a game force, so there is no need to jump).

(2)
SOUTH:	♠ K 7 5	♡ K 6 3	◇ A Q 9 2	♣ A 8 7

SOUTH	NORTH
1NT	2◇
2NT	3♠ (a)
4◇ (b)	6♠ (c)

(a) It is best to show the major suit early to avoid confusion. The non-jump bid leaves the way open for more exploration.

(b) Any bid other than three notrump or four spades at this point is encouraging. With practically all his values in aces and kings, South encourages by showing an ace. He chooses diamonds over clubs because he has a supporting honor in the former.

(c) Slam should be a good bet. North might invite the slam by bidding five spades, in which case South would co-operate by raising to six.

(3)
SOUTH:	♠ J 7 5	♡ A 6 3	◇ A 10 8	♣ K Q J 6

SOUTH	NORTH
1NT	2◇
2♡	2♠ (a)
2NT (b)	4♠ (c)
Pass (d)	

(a) South has denied the spade king, so slam is unlikely. Nonetheless, North leaves room for further dialogue.
(b) Showing that the two unbid suits are stopped.
(c) Settling for game. For all North can tell, the jack, as well as the king, of spades is missing.
(d) Nothing extra for slam purposes, so South subsides.

(4) NORTH: ♠ A Q J 10 6   ♡ A 8   ◇ 7   ♣ Q 10 6 4 2
     SOUTH: ♠ 9 7   ♡ K Q 5 2   ◇ A J 6 2   ♣ A K 5

SOUTH	NORTH
1NT	2◇
2♡	2♠
2NT (a)	3♣ (b)
3◇ (c)	4♣ (d)
5♣ (e)	6♣ (f)

(a) Clubs and diamonds are stopped; this bid leaves room to "look around."
(b) Value in clubs; may or may not be a suit.
(c) Maximum hand, good fit for clubs, diamond ace.
(d) Confirming a black two suiter.
(e) Showing extra club values.
(f) Bidding the odds-on slam.

WITH 5–4–2–2 HANDS

Clearly the two-diamond convention becomes more flexible when we drop the requirement for a 5-card minor suit. You might wonder whether we might also discard the condition of a side singleton or void. It can't be done, though, for it disturbs the solid foundation of the convention. Thus when holding 5–4–2–2 responder must take a shot at bidding three notrump directly or else bidding two clubs, Stayman, en route. There is no sure treatment for these hands; the more you explore, the more you tell the enemy. You have to decide whether you want to smash to game or try to set up a camouflage. In these decisions, we lean to the devious course, perhaps because it is one of bridge's greatest thrills to bamboozle the enemy.

WITH LESS THAN 11 POINTS

When responder has somewhat less than 11 points, he cannot resort to the two-diamond convention, even though the rest of his hand qualifies for the bid. Generally the best bet will be to bid three notrump immediately like the country cousin, hoping for a lucky fit or opening lead to bring you home free.

It doesn't pay to fool around when the opponents might have enough to butt in. Be happy that you've gotten past one opponent and take the opportunity to shut the other out. If the defense has a marked opening lead that beats the contract, you cannot help yourself; at least you haven't helped them. The direct raise to three notrump leaves the defense guessing when there is no marked lead. Simple bidding usually pays off. If you're taking a gamble, at least give yourself the best odds.

In contrast, you can afford to mess around to fool the enemy with 11 points or more. If they come in, the water's fine: either you will punish them with a double or go your own way and use the gratuitous information of the interference bid to your advantage in the play of the hand.

ASIDE TO DUPLICATE PLAYERS

At match points or board-a-match, we recommend you rein in the explorer instincts stimulated by the two-diamond convention. Unless you smell a slam, you had better settle for three notrump with the rest of the field. Even if you go down, you'll have company and will escape a bottom score.

The table of rewards at match play encourages adventures in notrump. It can be heartbreaking to arrive at an optimum five-diamond contract, score an overtrick by inspired play and then find that everybody else is playing an "unmakable" three notrump, but making four because the weak suit blocks! So we warn you in advance: don't write *us* about your troubles!

Perhaps as compensation, the Stayman *two-club* convention is even more applicable to match play than it is to rubber bridge. Successful tournament players look for a suit fit even with a 4-card major headed by a five-spot. In rubber bridge, this is losing tactics, for there may be nine running tricks at notrump, while a 4–1 trump split defeats the major-suit game. At match points though, four of a major counts for more than three notrump and it is worthwhile to take risks for the extra 20 points—and top on the board. When trumps break badly, you haven't tossed away a game, but just the one board.

SUMMING UP

The two-diamond convention may seem complex, because it is a new concept and because it asks more of your thinking apparatus. But it is well worth the effort. Any device that keeps you out of unmakable game contracts and steers you into successful slams is a treasure.

En route, you have to reveal your hand more fully than when you use the Stayman two-club bid. The opponents will have a better idea of what is going on, and in this sense, the two-diamond convention suffers a disadvantage not shared by the two-club convention. But the two-diamond convention guarantees more strength in responder's hand, so even this fault is minimized: you can better afford to let the opponents listen in if your team has the bulk of the power.

REBUTTAL TO POINT-COUNTERS

Don't get us wrong: we're *against* sin and we're *for* point count. But points are no substitute for reasoning. Since many players cannot comprehend how you can get to successful slams without 33 points, we had better translate the minor-suit slams we are espousing into point-count terms. As a matter of fact, the following analysis should help all players, of whatever degree of skill, in their slam quests.

THE THREE-SUIT DECK

The two-diamond response announces a singleton or void. When opener denies a stopper in that suit, a marked readjustment in point count is in order. In effect, you throw out that suit for point-count purposes. Instead of a four-suit deck totaling 40 points, imagine you are playing with a three-suit deck, hence a total of 30 points.

Let's say you are responder with a singleton spot card in spades and the bidding has gone:

SOUTH	NORTH
1NT	2◊
2♡	

Assume the worst—that partner has only 15 points and 2 of them are wasted in spades. That leaves him 13 points in the three-suit deck. You have a minimum of 11. *Voilà*, you have 24 points out of 30. If you can get the total up to 27, either by extra values in either hand or exceptional fit, then the most the opponents can have in your three-suit deck is a king. You have one spade loser—but only one. You want to be in a slam if that depends upon nothing more than a finesse. What—a slam on only 27 points? Yes, indeed.

And if you have a void with the same bidding, why then there is no spade loser and a mere 23 points may do the trick. The most the opponents can have is an ace and a king in your three-suit deck, and unless you are the unlucky sort who finds them both in the same suit *and* in the opening leader's hand, you should have a good enough play for that slam bonus.

We could go back over every hand in this section, applying this yardstick, but we think you will find it more rewarding discovering this new dimension by yourself. Happy Slam Hunting!

♠ 12 THE WEAK NOTRUMP

BIDDING ACCURACY improves in almost direct ratio to the frequency with which you use the precise and stable opening one-notrump bid. When vulnerable, it is dangerous to tamper much with the requirements. In Chapter 10, we championed the case for lowering the point range a notch to 15–17. Anything below that risks a substantial loss in search of a small gain.

THE NONVULNERABLE WEAK NOTRUMP

But when not vulnerable, you can afford to live more dangerously. We recommend a 12-to-14-point range—exactly 3 points lower than the strong notrump prescribed for vulnerable hands. Since you hold many more 12-to-14-point hands than 15-to-17-pointers in your lifetime, you have many more opportunities to open one notrump. But an even greater advantage is that the weak notrump shuts the opponents out of the one level. To accomplish this on a mere 12 points is a remarkable feat. To illustrate, you hold this hand, nonvulnerable against vulnerable opponents:

♠ A 7 5　♡ K 9 7 5　◊ 9 8　♣ A Q 7 6

The customary opening is one club, but this permits your left-hand opponent to sneak in on a borderline hand with any of four bids at the one level. After a weak notrump, however, he has to compete at the two level, which could be a holocaust if your partner is moderately stocked with goodies. (The weak notrump, like its strong older brother, is predicated on balanced shape and strength, so that partner can judge the doubling possibilities nicely.)

THE VULNERABILITY SCALE

There are just four vulnerability combinations:

	YOU	THEY
(1)	Nonvulnerable	Nonvulnerable
(2)	Vulnerable	Vulnerable
(3)	Vulnerable	Nonvulnerable
(4)	Nonvulnerable	Vulnerable

In bridge parlance, (1) and (2) are known as "equal vulnerability," (3) as "unfavorable vulnerability" and (4) as "favorable vulnerability." These terms indicate the relative climate for coming in with shaded overcalls or pre-emptive bids. Combination (3) is unfavorable because you can get clipped for a sizable penalty that far exceeds the value of the opponents' part-score or game. On the same reasoning, you have the advantage in (4), which is the ideal time for pre-emptive action—and therefore for the weak notrump. It can be very vexing for the opponents; yet they are reluctant to double for what might be a small penalty when they suspect they might have the makings of a vulnerable game.

WHEN TO USE THE WEAK NOTRUMP

Theoretically, you could use the weak notrump only with "favorable vulnerability," but that occurs only one-fourth of the time. At the other extreme you might employ a "three-quarter" weak notrump—in all situations except unfavorable vulnerability. However, you can get badly hurt when your partner is weak and the opponents double. One such debacle may outweigh the good results you pile up the rest of the time with the weak notrump.

Therefore our recommendation is to take a middle course and use the weak notrump half the time—whenever you are not vulnerable: (1) and (4). This compromise has the added advantage of simplicity. If you have ever had the experience of playing opposite a partner who forgot which kind of notrump the vulnerability specified, you will know exactly what we mean. For those who have escaped this fate, allow us to enumerate the possibilities: first, you missed a cold game or slam; second, you got clobbered at an impossible game or slam contract, usually doubled; or third, you somehow landed on your feet. The third is very rare indeed.

REQUIREMENTS FOR THE WEAK NOTRUMP

In adopting the weak notrump almost the only change is the point range. The other requirements noted under the strong notrump still prevail. Thus the hand must have:

1. A balanced shape (4-4-3-2, 4-3-3-3 or 5-3-3-2, but in the last case, open one in a major suit as good as K J x x x).
2. High cards in three suits.
3. 12-14 points.

Here are some typical hands that qualify:

(1)	♠ K 10 7 5	♡ A 8 6 2	◇ 6 4	♣ A K 9
(2)	♠ K 5 4	♡ Q 10 7 3	◇ J 2	♣ A K 8 3
(3)	♠ K J 4	♡ K 9 6	◇ A 8 7 6 3	♣ J 2

(1) is a maximum, (2) average and (3) minimum.

THIRD HAND

After two passes, it is often effective to open a notrump on a subminimum hand. It is also tempting to abuse the privilege, so we've set up three inhibiting guard ropes and shade the requirements only when (1) the vulnerability is favorable, (2) the hand counts to 11 high-card points (remember a 10-point hand is, after all, dead average) and (3) we have a 5- or 6-card escape suit—just in case the opponents get around to doubling.

Here is a hand that warrants a tactical one-notrump bid in third position with favorable vulnerability:

♠ 9 7 ♡ A Q 5 ◇ K 10 8 6 3 ♣ Q 6 4.

HOW RESPONSES ARE AFFECTED

The lower point-count requirements dictate some changes in responder's approach, for he no longer has the solid bulwark of 15 points opposite him. There are five adjustments he must make:

1. RESPONDER BIDS GAME WITH 12 POINTS

This may result in reaching game with a combined count of only 24 points, but the odds are in your favor. The even distribution of strength between the two hands facilitates transportation back and forth. The same balance often garners a cheap trick on the opening lead. When the bidding goes one notrump–three notrump, no information has been given away to the opponents and they frequently guess wrong on the opening lead. Don't worry about running into close penalty doubles either; for all either defender knows, the jump to three notrump could be based on 17 points as easily as on 12. The opponents are in the dark and are not apt to double rashly.

This protective umbrella also allows you to jump to three notrump on an unbalanced hand with a long minor suit. For example:

♠ 8 ♡ K 7 4 ◇ A Q 10 7 5 3 ♣ J 10 6.

Actually this hand counts to 12 points if you include the 2 distributional points for the diamond length.

2. RESPONDER DOESN'T USE TWO NOTRUMP AS AN INVITATION TO GAME

We've just seen how an immediate jump to a notrump game conceals responder's strength. Conversely, if you bid two notrump to invite game with, say, 11 points, you give the show away. Assume opener has a full 14 points and takes you to game; the opponents can be sure that you have just 25 points between you and no more. Whenever one of them has an establishable suit and a side entry, he can double with impunity. The bidding marks his partner with enough stoppers so that you won't roll three notrump with overtricks. Furthermore, the doubler knows that you don't have any reserve strength left for a redouble.

And what if your partner has a minimum and passes two notrump with a bare 12 points? An enterprising opponent might smell a nice penalty and double anyway.

No, our advice is to pass the balanced 11-point hands—and quickly. An unexpected dividend is that when the bidding goes

SOUTH	WEST	NORTH
1NT	Pass	Pass

East is put to a guess. He can't tell whether you have 11 points—or none—or somewhere in between. If he takes action, you can rough him up a bit with 11 points. If he stays silent, he might be missing a juicy penalty or contract of his own.

THE EXCEPTION

There is one time when it makes sense to use two notrump as a game invitation—and that is after a third-hand opening weak notrump. Responder cannot tell whether opener in this position has shaded his bid or has full values. So instead of jumping to three notrump with 12 points, he gives his partner leeway and invites game.

Therefore in this sequence:

NORTH	EAST	SOUTH	WEST
Pass	Pass	1NT	Pass
2NT	Pass		

North's bid shows 12 points (repeat 12, not 11) and asks opener to bid three notrump if he has not made a shaded third-hand bid. When South has bid a tactical notrump, he either passes over two notrump or takes out to three in his prepared escape suit—whichever he feels will play better. Thus, a suit rebid by South at the three level is an unequivocal sign-off and calls for a quick pass from North. A few examples will illustrate. In each case, the bidding has gone as in the diagram above, and you, South, hold the hand shown. What do you bid?

(1) ♠ Q 6 4 ♡ J 7 5 ◇ 9 8 ♣ A K J 7 5. *Pass.* Two notrump should make if the clubs run. If they do not, then three clubs will probably be down also. So there is no advantage to taking out into clubs.

(2) ♠ A 9 ♡ 10 6 ◇ Q 8 3 ♣ K J 10 8 6 3. *Bid three clubs.* You have a fair chance to make it. But you'll need a little club help from partner to bring home two notrump; if he has the needed club material, one of the side suits may be wide open. For all you know both three clubs and two notrump may be good contracts—or impossible ones. But on balance three clubs is the better chance.

(3) ♠ K 9 7 ♡ A 10 7 4 ◇ K J 6 ♣ Q 10 3. *Bid three notrump.* Partner asked you to bid game with a full-value notrump, so yours not to reason why. This just goes to show that a weak notrump need not be shaded just because it is bid in third position.

3. A BETTER USE FOR THE RAISE TO TWO NOTRUMP

It would be foolish to discard the two-notrump raise entirely just because it won't do as a game invitation. Instead, we suggest the bid be used as the "unusual" notrump, asking partner to bid his better minor.

For example, after partner's weak notrump, bid two notrump with either of these hands:

(1)   ♠ K 4 ♡ 7 ◇ Q 10 7 6 4 ♣ K 7 4 3 2
(2)   ♠ 8   ♡ 6 ◇ 9 7 5 4 3 2 ♣ A Q J 7 5

Partner must now bid three in his better minor suit and, of course, you will pass.

Note that this usage conforms to the general theory that a bid which consumes bidding space quickly is pre-emptive—just as an immediate three-club or three-diamond response to an opening notrump is pre-emptive. Exploratory bids that conserve bidding room are appropriate when you feel your side has the balance of power and you need room to search out the best contract.

A collateral advantage of giving a new meaning to the notrump raise is that it leads you away from temptation. No longer can you bid two notrump as an invitation to game—and to a deadly double.

4. RESPONDER IS QUICK TO SCAMPER

With a very weak hand, responder is quick to scurry to the greater security of a suit contract. For example, with ♠ Q 10 9 7 5 ♡ 6 3 ◇ 8 5 4 ♣ K 10 8 he bids two spades opposite a weak notrump; opposite a *strong* notrump he would be satisfied to pass in a contract that figures to make. But the *objective* differs with the weak notrump: The hand belongs to the opponents and neither one notrump nor two spades figures to make. Two spades may be more playable, but the crucial point is that it does a better job of shutting the opponents out. If they come in at all, it now has to be at the three level. They may have a superb heart fit and never be able to get into the bidding; or, if they do come in, they have to guess whether game is in the cards or nine tricks is their limit.

In these situations, responder needs only a glance at his hand to realize the opponents have the balance of strength—and that is just the time to get busy to put them off stride.

Another compelling reason to take out into two of a suit is to escape a penalty double. Constrast these two bidding sequences:

	SOUTH	WEST	NORTH	EAST
(1)	1NT	Pass	Pass	Double
(2)	1NT	Pass	2♡	Double

In (1) East's double is clearly for business. East states that from where he sits, he likes the idea of defending against one notrump doubled. If West accepts this view, South is in for a rough time.

But in (2) is East doubling two hearts for takeout or for penalties? We prefer the first interpretation, but it can be played either way. Whichever way your opponents use the double deprives them of the other usage. They can't have their cake and eat it too. About half the time your suit takeout will create a difficult problem for the defense. They face no such problem when you meekly pass to one notrump, for a double of one notrump can have but one meaning. Once one notrump has been doubled as in (1), and the other defender passes, it's dollars to doughnuts that you'll be doubled in whatever escape suit you find: each opponent knows that the other is satisfied to defend against a doubled contract, which means they have the balance of power. But it's extremely difficult for the opponents to read each other's holding as well when responder takes out to two of a suit.

Of course, a bid by North gives West another chance to speak. But if West was mute at his first turn, how often will he find his voice after this auction:

SOUTH	WEST	NORTH	EAST
1NT	Pass	2♡	Pass
Pass	?		

It is true that West now knows North's hand is limited and East's is marked with some strength, but there still may not be any effective action that he can take. Offsetting the risk that West can now cause damage is the bidding room your bid has consumed.

This does not mean that North can be frivolous in moving out of one notrump. A takeout should have the security of a 5-card suit at least. With a weak hand and four cards in each major suit, responder can resort to Stayman, as we shall see. Remember a suit takeout also increases the number of tricks you've bargained for. You should have at least an even chance to pull in an extra trick in order to jack up the bidding this one extra level. If you have a balanced hand as responder, don't be so quick to run. Opener may be all set with a perfectly delightful escape suit of his own if, and when, the double comes. And if not, one notrump doubled may be the least costly contract; it usually is when your side has nothing better than 4–3 suit holdings. In any event, it is reckless folly to take out into a 4-card suit when partner may have only a doubleton in support. Stay put, and if the enemy does nail you with a double, you can always resort to the S.O.S. redouble (p. 156) if you are intent on finding your 4–3 fit.

OPENER HELPS OUT

But let's assume that responder has good and sufficient reason to take out into his own suit. Frequently opener can pitch in with a jolly thrust of his own:

SOUTH	WEST	NORTH	EAST
1NT	Pass	2♡	Pass
3♡			

South's three-heart bid is purely pre-emptive, designed to make West's life miserable. South might have:

♠ 86 ♡ A K 5 4 ◇ K 8 6 ♣ Q 5 4 2.

Three hearts will probably go down, even though you have a good trump fit. But when your side has a good trump fit, the odds favor the opponents having a fit of their own. You can almost smell it here, and if you leave East-West to their own devices, they're bound to pick up the scent. If their suit is spades—likely since North would use Stayman if he were 4–5 in the majors—better not let them find out, for they outrank you and may have better than half the deck besides.

In the rare cases when opener wants to invite a game, despite his partner's apparent weakness, he bids a new suit in which he has top-card strength.

The bidding has been:

SOUTH	WEST	NORTH	EAST
1NT	Pass	2♡	Pass
?			

You, South, hold:

(1) ♠ 5 4 ♡ A Q 8 4 ◇ A 9 6 ♣ A 10 4 3. *Bid three clubs.* This must be a game try, based on an excellent fit for partner's hearts and a maximum notrump. Since there are three suits to choose from, the one South picks indicates the location of his strength. He could equally rebid three diamonds, but it is an inferior action, for it permits North just two courses—four hearts to accept the game invitation or three hearts to refuse it. However, if South instead bids three clubs, North is able to rebid three diamonds to show values in that suit. Then, South can see that he fits his partner in both red suits and *jumps* to four hearts, knowing he will have a good play for it. In other words, South's three-club bid allows him to elicit information as well as supply it, and he may be able to make the final decision whether or not to bid game.

COMPETITION

If your partner's weak notrump runs into an overcall, you have the same options for competing as though you were playing the strong notrump. For a summary of the various possibilities, see pages 48–49. The general principle is that a bid of any new suit at the two level or a minor-suit bid at the three level is competitive; a cue-bid in the opponent's suit or a bid in a new major at the three level is forcing.

5. NONFORCING STAYMAN

The need to run from one notrump with a weak hand is so pressing that it dictates a major change in the Stayman Convention. When playing the weak notrump, we switch over to the *nonforcing* variety of Stayman.

This simply means that opener is not forced to make another move over partner's rebid at the two level. The bidding can therefore die short of two notrump:

SOUTH	NORTH		SOUTH	NORTH
1NT	2♣	or	1NT	2♣
2◊	2♡ or 2♠		2♡	2♠
Pass			Pass	

Playing nonforcing Stayman, South is not forced to make another bid. In fact, he usually passes, since North's bidding confesses weakness. But South is allowed to exercise his own judgment. He may decide to raise partner's suit as a pre-emptive move; occasionally he will bid a new suit as a move toward game if he holds maximum values and a trump fit. But there is no obligation on South to bid further. That is the nub of nonforcing Stayman.

NONFORCING VERSUS FORCING STAYMAN

The concept of nonforcing Stayman will be clearer if we contrast it with *forcing* Stayman. A great amount of confusion surrounds this distinction. In our travels, the questions bridge players ask us most frequently are "What exactly is forcing Stayman?" and "What does it force to?"

Bridge players today are so accustomed to the idea of "game-forces" that many of them mistakenly think that forcing Stayman has to do with a commitment to game. Not so. Forcing Stayman sets up only a "one-round force" after which the bidding may die—and this force comes into play only in the two sequences diagrammed above: when responder, after bidding two clubs (Stayman), next bids a major suit at the two level. If forcing Stayman is in effect, opener must make another bid; if nonforcing Stayman is being played, he may pass.

It is difficult to lay down a short-cut rule of thumb to delineate between the two. The usual explanation we have heard for forcing Stayman is that after two clubs both partners are obligated to keep the bidding going until at least two notrump or three of a major has been reached. But this definition is misleading in two connections.

	SOUTH	NORTH
(1)	1NT	2♣
	2◊ , 2♡ , or 2♠	Pass!

We've heard players in the South seat protest that North cannot pass, for the pair is playing forcing Stayman. Nonsense! North has uncovered a better

part-score contract than one notrump and the last thing he wants is to hear
the bidding continue. So he passes. There is no force; the force, when it
comes, is after North's *second* bid at the two level; he has not made a
second bid here, ergo no force.

(2)	SOUTH	NORTH
	1NT	2♣
	2♦	3♡
	?	

If South interprets the usual definition of forcing Stayman in a literal
way, he might think he can pass over three hearts. After all, hasn't "three
of a major" been reached? True, but other considerations require South to
keep going: a bid of a new suit at the three level cannot be passed. A "forcing
situation" is created, all right, but it has nothing to do with forcing Stayman.
Bridge abounds with auctions in which a particular bid implies strength or
forces the bidding to keep going. The one that comes most readily to mind
is the cue-bid of an ace after a trump suit has been found; to pass your partner in a cue-bid is a heinous crime, so a forcing situation certainly exists.
But it has nothing to do with forcing Stayman. In short, the concept of a
forcing situation exists quite independently of the Stayman Convention, and
the forcing nature of bidding sequences that arise out of the Stayman Convention stand on their own merits.

WHEN DO YOU USE WHICH VARIETY?

We recommend forcing Stayman with the strong 15-to-17-point notrump
and nonforcing Stayman with the weak notrump. The distinction reflects
the difference in strength and purpose between the two kinds of notrump.

The strong notrump is oriented toward game contracts; the opening bid
itself guarantees that the pair has 60 percent of the strength needed for game
at the outset. Therefore every opportunity for game exploration is built into
the subsequent bidding. The forcing factor serves that purpose, for it puts
the partnership at ease; both partners can bid economically without jumping
prematurely. Thus they can investigate game chances while keeping the bidding low. Of course, there is a limit to how high you can force the bidding.
If, for example, you played that a two-club bid forced the pair to game,
why then you couldn't use the two-club bid on thousands of hands that
might produce game but depend upon partner having a suit fit or maximum
values. The most efficient method yet devised is to drop the force when two
notrump has been reached, allowing either partner to subside at that point.
This permits the maximum maneuverability: both partners can look for
game and still settle for part-score if they are discouraged in their search.

The *weak* notrump is a pre-emptive tool oriented to part-score competition. Therefore Stayman must serve a different purpose—giving responder one more means of scampering out of notrump into a more playable suit at the two level. Responder needs room to get out from under. But he can't use the convention if partner is obliged to keep the bidding going. That's the last thing he wants. So nonforcing Stayman is the answer. It assists in finding the best part-score. But to achieve this advantage you have to give up something: you lose the luxury of easy communication in quest of game at the two level, which is the hallmark of forcing Stayman. Of course, nonforcing Stayman can still get you to game after an opening weak notrump, but responder no longer has the tools to *invite* game, as the invitational bids have been transferred to the part-score arsenal.

In short, forcing Stayman, as played with the strong notrump, gives up a little in the area of part-score exploration in order to make sure of getting to good close games. On the other hand, nonforcing Stayman used with the weak notrump surrenders the invitational aspect on such hands to achieve more flexibility in the battle for part-scores.

THIRD AND FOURTH HANDS

We've had good success in using nonforcing Stayman in one additional situation—after a third- or fourth-hand *strong* notrump opening:

NORTH	EAST	SOUTH	WEST
Pass	Pass	1NT	Pass
2♣	Pass	2◇	Pass
2♡ or 2♠			

or

NORTH	EAST	SOUTH	WEST
Pass	Pass	1NT	Pass
2♣	Pass	2♡	Pass
2♠			

Since North couldn't open, chances for game are somewhat reduced. Generally passed hands bid more aggressively on the second round since their strength is limited and they must overcome the impression of weakness of the original pass. So North might force to game with a little less than otherwise; furthermore slam is so remote that the entire gamut of delicate inferential invitational bids is no longer required. How logical then to use nonforcing Stayman but as an invitation in this situation. North's message is: "I want to be in game if you have either a fit for my 5-card suit or a maximum notrump." South then (1) raises to four of the major with 3-card support and better than a minimum notrump, (2) raises to three of the major with 3-card support and a minimum notrump, (3) bids two notrump with better than a minimum notrump and a doubleton in support or (4) passes when he has the double flaw of a minimum notrump and only a doubleton in support of partner's suit. The advantage occurs in this fourth case, for the hand may make only eight tricks, and under forcing Stayman there is no way to invite game and still stop at two of a major.

This fourth situation occurs infrequently, so in this variation of nonforcing Stayman, it is rare that opener passes at the two level. In contrast, when playing nonforcing Stayman combined with the weak notrump, it is very rare for opener to go on bidding.

NONFORCING STAYMAN
AND THE WEAK NOTRUMP IN ACTION

To return to our central theme, let's observe nonforcing Stayman in operation with the weak notrump. When responder has 5–4 or 4–4 in the majors and a weak hand, it enables him to search out a better contract while making it difficult for the opponents to compete. But it is not a panacea for all weak hands. Responder must be ready for opener's response even if it is not to his liking. Responder should use nonforcing Stayman only when he has as good as 2-to-1 odds in his favor—in other words, when he is prepared to pass after two of partner's three possible rebids. But this encompasses a wide variety of holdings: four cards in both majors, one 4-card major and a tolerance for diamonds, or a 5-card major with some tolerance for an alternate contract.

The bidding has been

SOUTH	NORTH
1NT	?

and you, North, hold:

(1) ♠ J 7 4 ♡ K 9 7 3 ◇ A 8 6 5 3 ♣ 10. *Bid two clubs,* and pass partner's rebid. Either two diamonds or two hearts is a fine contract and even two spades—with a 4–3 fit—is superior to one notrump.

(2) ♠ Q 10 8 4 ♡ K 7 3 ◇ Q J 6 4 ♣ 9 7. *Pass.* Here again you would be happy to play in any suit partner bids over two clubs. But this time you have a balanced hand, so there's less urgency to run from notrump, even though it may not be the ideal contract. If the offensive capabilities were the only factor, two clubs would be the standout bid. But the defensive factor tips the scale toward a pass: if you pass, you have only one more opponent to get by, while a two-club bid allows both opponents another whack.

One sequence deserves special attention:

SOUTH	NORTH
1NT	2♣
2◇	2♡

In forcing Stayman, North promises a 5-card heart suit, but that is a luxury we can ill afford with the weak notrump. North may have compelling reasons for running from one notrump, as we have seen. Our system must allow him to scramble with two 4-card majors on a hand like

♠ Q 10 7 3 ♡ K J 6 3 ◇ 9 ♣ 8 7 5 2.

And what is he to do after partner replies two diamonds to his Stayman inquiry? Pass? No, his only sensible course is to bid the cheaper major as the most flexible call. Thus in this sequence North may have only four hearts, but he guarantees four cards in spades. Note how this requirement leads to an expert auction with these hands:

| NORTH: | ♠ Q 10 7 3 | ♡ K J 6 3 | ◇ 9 | ♣ 8 7 5 2 |
| SOUTH: | ♠ A J 6 | ♡ Q 8 | ◇ A 8 6 2 | ♣ Q 10 6 3 |

The bidding:

SOUTH	NORTH
1NT	2♣
2◇	2♡
2♠	Pass

South cannot be certain that his partner has five hearts, but he knows for a fact that he holds four spades. South therefore makes a master bid that caters to the possibility that North is 4-4 in the majors. He is thus assured that the partnership has found a 4-3 major fit. Perhaps North had five hearts, in which case he has given up a 5-2 fit for a 4-3 fit, but that is less of a misfortune than playing in a heart contract with the actual 4-2 distribution. Notice that South cannot make the corrective bid of two spades if his partner is apt to bid the same way without two 4-card majors.

OPENER IS NOT BARRED

Usually opener will pass a rebid of two in a major suit following responder's two-club inquiry. We have just seen a most unusual case of further action by opener, but there are two other more common circumstances which impel opener to make another move.

With a maximum notrump and a fine fit with partner, opener bids a new suit in which he has side strength. For example, if the bidding has gone:

SOUTH	NORTH
1NT	2♣
2◊	2♡
?	

and you, South, hold:

(1) ♠ A 5 ♡ K Q 7 ◊ A J 5 2 ♣ 6 5 4 2. *Bid three diamonds.* You have a maximum notrump and excellent support for partner's suit. The way to show this is to bid a side suit in which you have strength, thereby inviting game. (Note that you cannot bid two spades, for that would show dissatisfaction with hearts, as seen in the previous hand.) If partner declines the invitation by rebidding three hearts, you will of course pass.

With a good fit and fear that the opponents have a fit of their own, you can raise partner's suit as a pre-emptive effort. If the bidding, again, has gone:

SOUTH	NORTH
1NT	2♣
2◊	2♡
?	

and you, South, hold:

(2) ♠ 6 5 ♡ K Q 4 ◊ Q 7 5 ♣ A J 10 9 8. *Bid three hearts.* The opponents could easily have a good spade or diamond fit and more than half the deck between them. If partner is short in diamonds and has some help for your clubs, you should have a good play for three hearts. Even if you go down a trick, there's no loss if the opponents could have made a spade or diamond contract.

RESPONDER CAN'T INVITE GAME

It is comparatively rare that opener will find another bid after responder's rebid following Stayman. Most of the time responder will be left to play in two of his suit. In effect, then, responder cannot invite game; he may be able to accept opener's invitation if it is proffered. Otherwise he has to choose between playing at the two level or committing the partnership to game. There is no middle ground. This is the second time we have lost an invitational bid from our repertoire as a consequence of adopting the weak notrump; the other was the raise to two notrump discussed earlier.*

---

*Still a third such situation exists when responder holds a 6-card major suit. Even when playing the strong notrump, it is unwise to invite game with this holding. If you bid up to game gradually, the enemy knows you have no surplus strength and can double when they see that bad breaks are in store for you. So either bid game immediately—with apparent confidence, to avoid the double—or give up game and bid two of your suit.

GETTING TO GAME VIA STAYMAN

The weak notrump is best used as a general directional system. Responder tends to get to game quickly to play undoubled and depend on the luck of the fit and the opening lead to get him home. It is easy enough to get to game when responder has the equivalent of 12 points or more. After bidding two clubs, he can force to game by jumping to three in a 5-card major suit. Alternatively, he can probe for a suit fit by rebidding three clubs or three diamonds. Just as with the strong notrump, these bids set up game forces. Of course, if responder decides he doesn't want any more information from partner and wants to play at three notrump, he bids it at his second turn.

Note when responder commits the partnership to game, he makes no guarantee about his major-suit holding. Thus in this auction:

SOUTH	NORTH
1NT	2♣
2♠	3NT

South should *not* bid four hearts holding

♠ A J 6 4 ♡ Q J 7 6 ◇ K 5 ♣ K 5 3.

For all South knows, North may not have been serious about the majors and may have been laying a smoke screen to mislead the opponents. He might hold something like

♠ 7 ♡ K 8 4 ◇ A Q 10 7 4 2 ♣ J 10 6.

His tactics may discourage East from finding a spade lead against three notrump, and he won't be happy if you hang him for his effort by bidding four hearts. Remember that partner has the option of rebidding three clubs or three diamonds if he wants to learn more about your heart holding.

TWO DIAMONDS FOR MINORS

The two-diamond convention for minors plays very well with the weak notrump. In fact, we think it is even more valuable here. You get to open weak notrumps more often than the strong variety; therefore the convention gets you to good minor-suit games and slams that much more often. Furthermore, the weak notrump doesn't provide the blanket protection of stoppers in at least three suits; it only promises "high cards"—so there is greater danger of an unstopped suit if you bid a notrump game. Consequently there is more reason to ask about stoppers.

Since the range of the weak notrump is 3 points lower than the strong notrump, you need 3 more points to commit the partnership to game. So you show a minimum of 14 points, instead of 11, by a two-diamond response.

Opener's rebids are the same: two hearts shows a good heart stopper; two spades, a good spade stopper; two notrump, both major suits stopped. But a fourth response is now possible:

SOUTH	NORTH
1NT	2♢
3♣ or 3♢	

Before reading further, see if you can figure out the meaning.

OK, got it? South cannot have a good stopper in either major, so his notrump is likely to be based on a long, strong minor, the one he bid on the second round. He should bid three clubs on something like:

♠ 8 4 ♡ Q 4 ♢ K 9 7 ♣ A K J 6 5 3.

If North's singleton is in a major suit, he'll proceed to a minor-suit game or slam. But if it is in a minor suit, his best shot is three notrump.

HANDLING THE "STRONG NOTRUMP" HANDS

During your bridge career you will be dealt a number of balanced hands in the 15-to-17-point range, and you will smile inwardly, for you're 60 percent of the way to game. Before the days of the weak notrump you would simply utter the descriptive words, "One notrump." But if you have adopted the weak notrump, you will have to find another way to describe your hand when not vulnerable. Fortunately there is a simple solution: open one in a minor suit and rebid one notrump, thus:

SOUTH	NORTH
1♣ or 1♢	1♡ or 1♠
1NT	

In the old days this would show a minimum balanced hand, but now the weak notrump conveys that message, so the rebid of one notrump must show a better hand. (Of course, holding 18 or more points, a jump in notrump is in order.)

At first glance, this wrinkle seems to restrict the bidding. "What do I bid if my natural rebid would have been one notrump?" Look again: shouldn't you have opened with a weak notrump, which would have eliminated the rebid problem? No? Then the hand did not qualify for one of two reasons: either it was (1) unbalanced or (2) it had high cards in less than three suits. In either case, a suit rebid is more descriptive, so that is the bid to make.

RESPONDER'S ACTION AFTER A NOTRUMP REBID

In general, responder bids just as if the opening bid had been a strong notrump. After this start:

SOUTH	NORTH
1♣	1♠
1NT	

NORTH'S REBID	HAS THIS MEANING
2♠	A desire to play at 2♠
2◊ or 2♡	Shows a two suiter, not forcing on South
3 in any suit	Natural bid, forcing to game
2NT	Asks opener to bid 3NT with more than a minimum

TWO CLUBS FOR STAYMAN

The two-club bid is reserved for Stayman:

	SOUTH	NORTH
(1)	1♣ or 1◊	1◊, 1♡ or 1♠
	1NT	2♣

This is most logical, for South has shown the values for an opening strong notrump, and North must be given the facilities for investigating the major suits. Thus the situation is almost identical with:

	SOUTH	NORTH
(2)	1NT	2♣
	(strong)	

There are a few subtle differences between the two auctions, however. In (1) North has shown enough values to keep the bidding open and the partnership has already named two suits. Since the auction has illumined several features of the partnership holding, a Stayman two-club bid at this juncture logically shows game interest. It behooves South to clarify his hand and he may have to go beyond the two-notrump level to show a maximum. In effect, neither "forcing" nor "nonforcing" Stayman is used, but rather a hybrid, as the following sequences will show.

After this start:

SOUTH	NORTH
1♣	1♠
1NT	2♣

1. South with a minimum 15 points bids:
   A. Two hearts to to show a biddable 4-card heart holding.
   B. Two spades to show no biddable 4-card heart holding, but a 3-card spade suit. (South should have raised spades immediately, in preference to a notrump rebid, if he held four cards in the suit, so this "delayed preference" must show a 3-card holding.)
   C. Two diamonds to show neither a biddable 4-card heart suit nor 3-card spade support.
2. South with better than a minimum 15 points bids:
   A. Three hearts to show a biddable 4-card heart holding.
   B. Three spades to show no 4-card heart holding, but 3-card spade support.
   C. Three clubs or three diamonds to show he has neither a biddable 4-card heart holding nor 3-card spade support, but side strength in the bid minor.
   D. Two notrump—same as C. but with no particular preference in the minors. (With an absolute maximum, South might rebid three notrump, but in most cases South should prefer two notrump, as it gives partner more room; rarely will North drop the bidding at two notrump, and if he does, there's probably an inferior play for game.)

AFTER A HEART RESPONSE

Thus far we have put a spade bid in North's mouth on the first round. If he bids hearts instead, we have two more possible auctions:

	SOUTH	NORTH
(1)	1♣ or 1◇	1♡
	1NT	2♠

A reverse by responder is forcing to game. North may be 4–4 or 4–5 in the majors.

	SOUTH	NORTH
(2)	1♣ or 1◇	1♡
	1NT	2♣
	2♠	

Opener not only shows four spades but better than a minimum hand, for his bid forces North to the three level if he doesn't have spade support.

AN AMBIGUOUS SEQUENCE

We have not covered the sequence

SOUTH	NORTH
1♡	1♠
1NT	

before, for it is an ambiguous one. Since the bidding started at the upper edge of the one level, it would constrict South to require him to bid at the two level just to show a minimum hand. Therefore South should be allowed to rebid one notrump with less than 15 points. But equally he may be in the 15-to-17-point range. It is therefore best to leave the one-notrump rebid in this sequence as a "two-way" action. If responder is interested in knowing opener's strength, he can use Stayman in an extended sense:

SOUTH	NORTH
1♡	1♠
1NT	2♣

If South bids two of any suit, he indicates less than 15 points. Any other bid pinpoints him in the 15-to-17-point range.

WEAK NOTRUMP—PRO AND CON

The weak notrump is fun to play and gets you into the bidding more often. It also gives you an opportunity to scramble and scrap for part-scores and thus we recommend it for aggressive players. But whether or not you decide to adopt it yourself you should be familiar with its workings, for you will surely have to defend against it some time or other. And that brings us to our next chapter.

⟨13⟩ DEFENSE AGAINST

THE WEAK NOTRUMP

THE WEAK NOTRUMP is designed as a pre-emptive, obstructive tool and it sacrifices accuracy to achieve these ends. We have observed that responder has ample opportunities to muddy the waters and make things difficult for the defense. How then can the defense chart its course?

THE TWO-CLUB OVERCALL

Ordinarily any two-level overcall of an opening notrump is a natural bid showing a genuine suit. However, the defense needs more flexibility to combat the pre-emptive value of the weak notrump. Therefore a two-club overcall over a weak notrump has come to be an artificial bid, asking partner to name his better major suit. It does the same job for the defense that Stayman does for opener's side. In the United States this convention is frequently called Landy, after the Secretary of the American Contract Bridge League, Alvin Landy, who helped develop it.

A "SAFE" TAKEOUT DOUBLE

In effect, the two-club overcall is a takeout double that partner cannot pass. It gives the defense a second string to its bow, for the double is still available to portray a hand of opening-bid strength. Since a weak notrump may be bid with as many as 14 points, it is hazardous to double without at least 14 points. Of course, a double can be made on more than this—for this is virtually the only strong defensive call on a balanced hand—but it should rarely be made on less. An exception occurs when the opening one-notrump bid has been passed by the next two players. Then the fourth player can shade his double a bit, for he does not have to contend with the problem of the opening lead. If his partner does not have a good opening lead, he will give serious consideration to removing the double into his best suit.

THE DOUBLE VERSUS TWO CLUBS

A double is essentially for penalties, but partner has the option of taking out the double if he lacks defensive values and has a somewhat unbalanced hand. Two clubs, on the other hand, is exclusively for takeout. It is used to describe a hand with insufficient high-card strength to warrant a double. (Occasionally two clubs will be preferred on hands qualifying for the takeout double when there is no good lead against one notrump doubled.)

The two-club takeout abandons the defensive role and seeks out a playable contract with which to compete. It indicates a hand that is offensively strong in the major suits and usually weaker than 14 points in high cards. The two-club bid promises support for *both* major suits. Here is an example:

♠ K J 6 5 4 ♡ A 10 7 6 2 ♢ 8 ♣ Q 3.

This is a very powerful hand in distribution, although it contains but 10 high-card points, and can play well opposite partner's three small cards in one of the majors. Furthermore, if this hand is passed, the partnership will have no opportunity to exchange any information and it becomes a guess which major suit will be the more telling opening lead. But that is a subsidiary matter; the important consideration is that this hand is better suited for offense. Even if the best opening lead is found, the notrump contract may be made, while all the time the hand might produce a part-score the other way if partner's cooperation is sought. This is the kind of hand with which one must step out and find the part-score.

RESPONSES TO TWO CLUBS

The partner of the two-club bidder must bid his better major suit, even if it is only three cards long. The only excuse for failing to bid a major suit is a doubleton or worse in both major suits. In these cases, partner passes to two clubs with a long club suit and bids two diamonds with a long diamond suit.

EXAMPLES

The bidding has progressed:

SOUTH	WEST	NORTH	EAST
1NT	2♣	Pass	?

and you, East, hold:

(1) ♠ Q 7 6 ♡ 4 2 ◇ K 8 5 4 3 2 ♣ 8 4. *Bid two spades.* With a 3-card major suit you must not show the diamonds.

(2) ♠ Q 5 4 2 ♡ K 8 ◇ A 7 6 3 ♣ 8 5 2. *Bid three spades.* Partner has forced you to bid at the two level, no matter how weak your hand might be. Since you have a good 4-card spade suit, a fit in the other major suit and an outside ace, the hand warrants a strong invitation to game. (We would make the same bid if South were using a strong notrump, provided, of course, that we had agreed with partner that the two-club bid is artificial against the strong notrump, just as it is against the weak notrump.)

(3) ♠ Q 10 8 7 3 ♡ Q J 3 ◇ A 6 5 4 2 ♣ None. *Bid three clubs.* This is a cue-bid, forcing to game, for if East were weak and merely had a long club suit, he would pass the two-club overcall.

There might even be a slam in the hand. Pair this hand with the typical two-club overcall on page 148.

WEST	EAST
♠ K J 6 5 4	♠ Q 10 8 7 3
♡ A 10 7 6 2	♡ Q J 3
◇ 8	◇ A 6 5 4 2
♣ Q 3	♣ None

Six spades is a romp, provided that South has the king of hearts as part of his notrump bid.

IN FOURTH POSITION

When the bidding has gone one notrump-pass-pass, the two-club over-call retains its meaning; it is an artificial bid, asking for partner's better major suit. However, the bid is practically never made on more than 15 points. We pointed out earlier that the only reason for bidding two clubs on 15 points or more is when the hand presents a lead problem. But when partner is due to make the opening lead, this consideration no longer applies.

The whole purpose of bridge is to score on the plus side. A two-club over-call lets the opponents off the hook, while a double nails them to the mast. So if your hand qualifies for a double in fourth position, by all means make that bid.

THE SECOND TIME AROUND

Nowadays, a hand with 13 high-card points is rarely passed. Therefore, a double by a passed hand shows a lesser point count, bolstered by fine distribution in the majors. Instead, if two clubs is bid, it is a natural call, showing a club suit.

TWO CLUBS AGAINST A STRONG NOTRUMP

Thus far we have been discussing the artificial use of two clubs after a weak notrump. This is the historical treatment, as the bid was devised to combat the pre-emptive advantage of the weak notrump. However, leading players have found it equally effective against the strong notrump. The objective changes somewhat; you will rarely be able to score a game, but you may be able to outbid the opponents in the part-score contest or find a cheap save.

PREFER THE DIRECT APPROACH

You are East and the bidding has gone:

SOUTH	WEST	NORTH	EAST
1NT	Pass	Pass	?
(strong)			

You hold:

(1) ♠ K Q 10 9 6 4 ♥ J 7 4 2 ♦ A Q ♣ 8. *Bid two spades.* Technically the hand qualifies for a two-club overcall. However, this gives South the opportunity to come in at the two level with a 5-card red suit with no corresponding advantage to your side; for, if West responded two hearts to your two-club overcall, you would still correct to two spades. Why not bid two spades directly? A two-spade part-score is very promising, and game is most unlikely.

The mere fact that you have a tool does not mean you must use it. The direct and natural approach is always preferable unless there is a clear-cut advantage in the indirect and artificial course. More on this in Chapter 14.

AFTER TWO NOTRUMP

The club overcall is also used in the artificial sense after an adverse opening bid of two notrump. A two-notrump opening is often bolstered by a long and strong minor suit; instead of being overawed by the strength announced by the bid, as defender, you should try to find a major-suit contract of your own—one that you can fulfill or one that represents a profitable save.

Example (North-South vulnerable):

NORTH
♠ 9 3
♡ 8 4 2
◊ Q 8 3
♣ Q J 6 5 2

WEST
♠ K 6 5 4 2
♡ K Q 10 9 6
◊ 7
♣ A 8

EAST
♠ Q 10 8 7
♡ 7 3
◊ J 9 5 2
♣ 10 9 4

SOUTH
♠ A J
♡ A J 5
◊ A K 10 6 4
♣ K 7 3

SOUTH	WEST	NORTH	EAST
2NT	3♣ (a)	3NT (b)	4♠ (c)

(a) West decides, correctly, to compete, rather than sit back complacent with his prospects of defeating a three-notrump contract.

(b) North tries to make things difficult for East and succeeds in shutting him out of the three level. A less enterprising North would make the "book" call—doubling three clubs to show where his strength was—but note that this would allow East to bid comfortably at the three level.

(c) Give East a real good mark for his four-spade bid. He appreciated that his near-Yarborough becomes a powerful hand on this auction. A holding of four cards in one major and a doubleton in the other must be just what his partner ordered. It supplies a dominant trump suit and the ruffing power to set up the long side suit.

Four spades goes down a trick—a fine sacrifice. But that is only part of the story. If West had not gotten into the bidding and if East had not made his enterprising bid, South would have bought the hand at three notrump.

And what would West have led? Remember, he has no clue to the spade situation. Surely the king of hearts would be his choice. Against that opening a competent declarer would make five notrump. He would recognize the danger of a spade shift at trick two and so would take the first trick with the heart ace. He would then proceed to knock out the club ace; and the odds are all in his favor. About the only way the hand could go down is if East had both the ace of clubs and exactly a doubleton heart. In the actual case, when West takes the ace of clubs, he has no defense to break the contract. On regaining the lead, South takes the safety play in diamonds—ace first and then over to the queen—and runs the entire suit by taking the marked finesse against East's jack.

RESPONDER STEALS YOUR BID

At times it seems as if an opening weak notrump sets up a battlefield in which each side races to be the first to bid an artificial two clubs. We have already seen how useful this artificial bid is to the defense; earlier we witnessed how a nonforcing two-club Stayman bid enables responder to wriggle out of an inferior contract.

Responder's two-club Stayman bid can be based on anything from a very weak to a robust hand. Thus, the auction conceals his strength until the last possible moment. To demonstrate, look at this sequence from the East-West vantage point:

SOUTH	WEST	NORTH	EAST
1NT	Pass (a)	2♣	Pass (b)
2◇	Pass (c)	2♠ (d)	

- (a) For all West knows, North may be lurking with 10, 15 or even 20 points. So it is folly for West to come in without the equivalent of a sound opening bid.
- (b) North's two-club bid may be the first step to a game, or even a slam contract, so East, having heard his partner's pass, won't venture forth with a borderline hand.
- (c) North's strength is still masked, so West is still effectively muzzled.
- (d) At last the cat is out of the bag: North does not have a game-going hand. But East still has to tread warily, for North may have as many as 11 points. By this time East-West have lost three opportunities to exchange information. It is less likely that an opponent will fight the odds by sticking in a bid now.

FIGHTING BACK

Much can be learned from the preceding example. First, if East-West compete at all, they must do so at the two level, for it is far more dangerous to wait until the bidding subsides and then come in at the three level. (Some experienced players subscribe to the theory of waiting until the opponents have had their say and then entering the bidding; this approach may work if you have a self-sufficient suit, but it is most hazardous if you must first try to find a fit with partner at a high level.)

North's two-club bid creates an elaborate smokescreen, for none of the other three players can gauge his strength at this point. Still, the fear is more apparent than real; if North is weak, then it is safe for East to contest the bidding; and if North is strong enough for game, East may do well to explore for a sacrifice.

But there is no doubt that North's bid is inconvenient to East-West. Without it, the auction would have gone one notrump-pass-pass and East has the choice of bidding two clubs himself or doubling. Now he has only the double left to express his hand.

A NEW MEANING FOR THE DOUBLE

Since East-West have been deprived of the two-club bid, the double has to carry more of the burden. Ordinarily, the double of an artificial bid shows length and strength in that suit and promises nothing extra in the rest of the hand. However, that interpretation restricts the opportunities for the double.

The double has much greater utility if it describes a hand that would have doubled one notrump had North passed. Used in this fashion, the double shows 14 high-card points or more and attempts to indicate the total North-South strength to partner so that he can take intelligent action. However, the double makes no statement whatsoever about the club suit.

SPIRITED COMPETITION

Here is a full hand to illustrate tactical stroke and counterstroke:

```
                    NORTH
                    ♠ J 6 4 3
                    ♡ Q 7 2
                    ◇ J 9 8 5
                    ♣ 7 3
    WEST                            EAST
    ♠ Q 10 9 2                      ♠ A K 8
    ♡ 9 6                           ♡ A J 5 3
    ◇ K 10 4 3                      ◇ 7 2
    ♣ A 9 5                         ♣ Q 10 8 6
                    SOUTH
                    ♠ 7 5
                    ♡ K 10 8 4
                    ◇ A Q 6
                    ♣ K J 4 2
```

If North were a run-of-the-mill player, the bidding would probably go:

SOUTH	WEST	NORTH	EAST
1NT (weak)	Pass	Pass	Double (a)
Pass	Pass (b)	Pass	

(a)   Invites West to pass for penalties.
(b)   West can count his side for over half the deck—not enough to score a game his way but, with the advantage of the opening lead, ample to set one notrump a few tricks. And that is exactly what happens.

Now let's take the same hand and assume that North is educated in the weak notrump:

SOUTH	WEST	NORTH	EAST
1NT (weak)	Pass	2♣ (a)	Double (b)
2♡	2♠ (c)		

(a)   North is quite sure that East will take some action if he passes, so he endeavors to cloak his weakness, planning to pass any rebid by opener. Note that he can stand a rebid of two spades, two hearts or two diamonds. Had he held a doubleton in any of these suits, he would have been ill advised to take any action on this extremely weak hand.
(b)   East takes the only available course—a double to show 14 points.
(c)   Pity poor West. Perhaps he should double two hearts, for he can count that his side has at least 23 points. But for all he knows, North-South may have an excellent heart fit and even make their contract. He would like to make a "tentative" double which his partner would pull out if he had nothing in hearts, but there is no such bid in the bridge lexicon. A pass is out of the question, for his partner will never know he has 9 points and is likely to sell out to the opponents undoubled. So West chooses the least-of-evils course, hoping to find a fit with partner and chalk up a part-score. But the hands do not fit that well and East-West earn a minus score, notwithstanding their 23 points and their progressive use of the double over two clubs.

DEFENSE AGAINST THE DEFENSE

As pointed out earlier, the side that bids the artificial two clubs first has the advantage. Thus, when *your* partner opens one notrump and the next player overcalls with two clubs, you can no longer bid two clubs (Stayman) yourself. Yet your hand may warrant fighting for the part-score. The ground rules were laid out in Chapter 5: a suit bid at the two level is competitive, as is a *minor* suit at the *three* level. But a *major* suit at the three level constitutes a game force.

These actions are based on 5-card or longer suits, which create no great problem. Difficulty arises when you have two or more 4-card suits and need partner's advice in placing the contract. Sometimes it is impossible to give partner a choice: in the previous hand West bid a 4-card suit as the most intelligent action and came to grief. The same fate can befall the other team just as easily.

No all-encompassing rule can be laid down to deal with these problems. Good judgment is needed, as you will see in the following three examples. In each case the bidding has progressed:

SOUTH	WEST	NORTH
1NT (strong)	2♣ (artificial)	?

and you, North, hold:

(1) ♠ 6 ♡ Q 9 6 ◇ 8 5 2 ♣ Q 10 8 6 4 3. *Bid three clubs—just as if there had been no overcall.* That is where you want to play the hand. This must be a natural bid; you cannot cue-bid a suit bid artificially by an opponent. You could double—this is the accepted way of showing strength in in a suit that is bid artificially—but what would be the point? You know that East-West will not land in clubs, so why not take the opportunity to deprive them of one round of bidding with which to find their fit? (Note that three clubs is the proper response even if South opened with a *weak* notrump.) *Caution:* if you are playing with a strange partner, better pass quietly, as he might mistakenly think three clubs is a cue-bid anyway.

(2) ♠ A Q 6 5 ♡ K J 6 2 ◇ 8 5 ♣ 8 5 3. *Bid three notrump.* Again you try to deprive the opponents of bidding room. You have the values for your bid, but you don't want East to bid a suit to indicate a favorable lead to his partner. Presumably West will try a major-suit opening, for which you are well prepared. The three-notrump call gives up any chance for a major-suit contract, but since West announced interest in the major suits, this is no great loss.

An alternate action would be to pass and then double any major suit that East bids. If he bids two diamonds, you can then cue-bid three diamonds to investigate the major suits. But remember, the waiting game is not always the winning game. If clubs is his best suit, East may very well pass his partner's artificial two-club overcall and North will be left redfaced.

(3) ♠ 6 5 ♡ 4 ◇ Q 10 8 4 2 ♣ Q J 7 5 3. *Bid three clubs or three diamonds.* Playing the strong notrump, you cannot give partner a choice of your minors. You cannot bid two notrump, for that would indicate a balanced hand of 8–9 points. But if you are playing weak notrump, bid two notrump with this hand. This bid has the same meaning as if there had been no intervention by West—a request for partner to bid his better minor suit—and has the same pre-emptive effect as an immediate three-club or three-diamond bid with the advantages of finding an 8-card trump suit and playing from the strong side.

OTHER INTERFERENCE

So far we've covered the situations where the opener's left-hand opponent competes with a Landy two-club bid. What happens if he instead bids a suit naturally:

SOUTH	WEST	NORTH
1NT	2♢, 2♡	?
	or 2 ♠	

If North is strong enough to insist on game, he simply cue-bids the opponent's suit:

SOUTH	WEST	NORTH
1NT	2♡	3♡

South should realize that Stayman was not available and bid the other major with 4-card length.

However, if North doesn't have the wherewithal to insist on game, he bids two notrump, irrespective of stoppers in the opponents' suit. Again, South should bid his 4-card major suit—*unless* he holds a minimum. With a minimum, a pass is preferred, just as if there had been no intervening bid. It is possible that a pass will result in the loss of the 4-4 major-suit fit, but this is a price that must be paid. Such is the power of pre-emption, even in a simple overcall.

THE S.O.S. REDOUBLE

Inevitably there are times when you are busted and your partner opens one notrump (and all too often, a *weak* notrump). This is a most uncomfortable turn of events, and all you can hope to do is limit your losses.

With a perfectly flat hand, you should pass and hope for the best. Holding a hand with some shape—at least 4-3 in the majors and at least three diamonds—you can try to confuse the opponents by bidding two clubs, Stayman, and then pass the response. This tactic often throws the enemy off stride and escapes a double.

An alternative is to pass the hand and wait for the ax to fall. When the double comes, an S.O.S. redouble is available to extricate yourself. The redouble asks partner to bid his lowest-ranking 4-card suit until a 4-3 (or hopefully 4-4) fit is found. Here is an example:

NORTH: ♠ Q 8 6 5 ♡ 10 7 5 4 ◇ 3 2   ♣ Q 8 6
SOUTH: ♠ K 3   ♡ K J 6 3   ◇ A Q 7 4 ♣ K 5 2

SOUTH	WEST	NORTH	EAST
1NT (strong)	Pass	Pass	Double
Pass	Pass	Redouble (a)	Pass
2◇ (b)	Pass	2♡ (c)	Pass
Pass (d)	Pass		

(a)   North sees his side has barely half the deck's high-card strength and his hand has no sure entry. One notrump doubled appears to be a miserable contract, so North tries to find a 4–3 suit fit. His redouble asks partner to bid his lowest 4-card suit.

(b)   South dutifully obliges.

(c)   If North had three diamonds, he would pass gratefully, but with a doubleton he must go on and bid his lowest 4-card suit, hearts.

(d)   This strikes gold and South is happy to pass. If South had three hearts, he would also pass; it is just luck that the partnership stumbled on a 4–4 fit.

The same S.O.S. redouble is available to the opening notrumper:

SOUTH	WEST	NORTH	EAST
1NT	Double	Pass	Pass
Redouble			

South knows he is in trouble and asks his partner to bail him out.

The S.O.S. redouble is a handy escape hatch, and the chances of finding a 4–3 fit are greatly in your favor. Before you become too enamored of this sparkling little gadget, think of the dire consequences if your partner does not understand the meaning of the redouble and blithely passes you in an impossible one notrump contract, doubled and redoubled! Better size up your partner before redoubling; a prompt pass by you may cut your losses in half!

WHEN A REDOUBLE IS NOT S.O.S.

There is one case—and one case only—where a redouble following a notrump is not for rescue. That is this auction:

SOUTH	WEST	NORTH
1NT	Double	Redouble

North's action shows a hand that is good enough to raise the opening bid if there had been no interference; thus he is perfectly content to play in one notrump redoubled and score an easy game with overtricks. More likely, though, East will run out to his best suit. North's redouble alerts South that his side has the balance of strength and South should double the opponents. As a safety measure, it is unwise to double with less than three trumps because it is just possible that the opponents will find an excellent fit and in that eventuality, North-South will want to bid their own game or part-score. Thus, if either North or South lacks three cards in the opponent's run-out suit, he should pass and hope his partner can double it.

AN IMPOSSIBLE AUCTION

But this is an impossible auction:

SOUTH	WEST	NORTH	EAST
1NT	Double	Redouble	Pass
Pass	2◊	Pass	Pass
Pass!			

If South cannot double two diamonds, he must make *some* bid. It is sheer foolishness to sell out to the opponents, undoubled, when your side has the preponderance of strength.

THE LOGIC OF IT ALL

The distinction between the S.O.S. redouble and the strength-showing redouble is logical. For example, in this auction:

SOUTH	WEST	NORTH	EAST
1NT	Pass	Pass	Double
Pass	Pass	Redouble	

North's redouble cannot show strength, for he has already passed over one notrump. It is only when the partner of the opening notrumper has not had a chance to respond that his redouble promises strength. Harking back to our previous point about partnership understanding, how many partners do you know who can be trusted to distinguish between the two redoubles?

Here is one last sequence to try on your favorite partner: what does the redouble mean?

NORTH	EAST	SOUTH	WEST
Pass	Pass	1NT	Double
Redouble			

The redouble shows strength. Just because North did not open the bidding doesn't mean he cannot have 10, 11 or 12 points. Note that he has not had a chance to *respond* to his partner's notrump; hence, the redouble shows real values.

YOU ARE NOT *FORCED* TO REDOUBLE

Failure to make a strength-showing redouble is no real solace to the opponents. Take this auction:

NORTH	EAST	SOUTH	WEST
Pass	Pass	1NT	Double
Pass	?		

East is not sure whether North was just short of a raise to two notrump or is bankrupt; he may have a pretty good hunch, judging by his own hand and the strength shown by South and West, but he still has to guess. If East passes, South may roll one notrump; if East bids a suit, North may be waiting with the ax. In short, even without the strength to redouble, you may get a chance for a delectable penalty double, or an easy doubled part-score.

THE NONVULNERABLE ONE-NOTRUMP OVERCALL

Since this chapter is mainly concerned with obstructive tactics and countermeasures to combat them, it seems an appropriate place to mention a new interpretation for the one-notrump overcall, nonvulnerable.

In Part I we recommended the notrump overcall for a balanced hand of 16–18 points (16 only if bolstered by a double stopper in the opponents' bid suit). This should not be shaded even when you adopt the 15-to-17-point range for the strong notrump; it is just too easy for your left-hand opponent to double a shaded notrump with an average holding—and if you or your partner decide to run out, it will have to be at the two level.

However, with favorable vulnerability, we recommend a two-way notrump overcall that permits you to interfere with the opponents' bidding on a long minor suit. The requirements are a strong 6- or 7-card suit in a hand that is slim in high cards, something like

♠ 5 ♡ 10 6 4 ◇ K Q 10 8 7 6 3 ♣ 7 5.

A notrump overcall can hinder the opponents' exchange more effectively than the weak jump overcall otherwise used on such a holding.

If partner is interested in finding out which kind of notrump overcall you have, he uses the Stayman two-club bid, whether or not he has interest in the majors. The bid now asks a different question from the usual. It inquires: "Do you have a real notrump, or are you kidding?" With a real 16-to 18-point notrump, the overcaller must rebid two notrump. Any suit bid—even a jump—is a confession that the notrump overcall was a tactical bid.

BUFFALOING THE OPPONENTS

Sometimes the overcaller's partner will have no reason to bid over one notrump and the notrump overcall may be followed by three passes with nobody the wiser. (Of course, this usage of the notrump overcall must be announced to opponents in advance, but it is sometimes difficult for them to tell whether the overcall is honest or not.)

If the opponents double one notrump, the overcaller's partner must not run out to some broken suit, for he might find only a singleton as support. The overcaller can run out into his long minor suit whenever his bid was tactical.

THE DISADVANTAGE

Anytime you use a bid in a specialized way, you have to give up something in return. In this variation, a two-notrump rebid by overcaller makes it impossible for responder to sign off at two of a major. Therefore, responder cannot bid two clubs with a weak hand and length in the majors. Furthermore, there is little sense in bidding over one notrump if you plan to pass to two notrump. Hence, the two-club response becomes forcing to game when the overcaller rebids two notrump, confirming a full-value notrump.

RESPONDER'S OPTIONS

However, responder can make a simple suit takeout at the two level, just as he would if he were sure the notrump was of the strong variety. No real harm can result: if the overcall was tactical, partner can pass with a doubleton or tripleton in the suit or take out to his own suit. Either way, the pre-emptive value of the tactical notrump bid has been enhanced: a bidding level has been stolen from the opponents before they discover the hoax.

Responder can also jump to three clubs or three diamonds, but he needs a fairly solid suit, for partner may have a singleton. However, a jump to three of a major is naive, for if partner has made a tactical bid, his suit is probably better than yours. And there is no such bid as three notrump over the notrump overcall. If you make the bid on 10–11 points, you'll go down a bundle whenever partner has bid tactically; and if you have enough to make game even opposite that kind of hand—say about 20 points—there is nothing to be gained by rushing the bidding. Bid two clubs first. If partner bids a suit, you can jump to three notrump on your next turn. But occasionally you'll hear a two-notrump rebid, and then you can go about the happy business of bidding your slam (there is no law prohibiting the opponents from opening a psychic!).

"READING" THE BIDDING

Responder has to be on his toes to figure out what's going on without giving the show away:

NORTH
♠ J 5 3
♡ Q 6 2
◇ A 7
♣ Q 10 9 4 3

WEST
♠ 8
♡ 10 7 4
◇ K Q 10 9 5 4 2
♣ 6 2

EAST
♠ A Q 9 7 6 4
♡ K 8 3
◇ J 8
♣ K 5

SOUTH
♠ K 10 2
♡ A J 9 5
◇ 6 3
♣ A J 8 7

SOUTH	WEST	NORTH	EAST
1♣	1NT (a)	2♣	2♠ (b)
3♣	Pass	Pass	Pass (c)

(a) The tactical notrump overcall.
(b) East smells something fishy. If his partner has an honest notrump, then North-South are doing an awful lot of bidding on 11 points. Still, it can't hurt to throw a little sand in their eyes and at the same time direct a lead.
(c) East continues his good work by a quick, quiet pass before the opponents can recover.

As it turns out, North-South can make three notrump: lucky with a combined count of 22 points? Yes, but we have all seen opponents helped into such lucky games by partners who simply cannot bring themselves to pass at the right time.

⟨14⟩ ARTIFICIALITY—

PRO AND CON

IT MAY COME as a surprise to read at this late stage that we are opposed to artificial bids in principle. Yet it is our firm conviction that whenever you bid to your final contract naturally and directly—and in as few steps as possible—you have a far better chance of success.

There is a greater ring of authority to auctions like one diamond–six diamonds or one spade–four spades than you will find in any other style of bidding. Moreover, these auctions give away a minimum of information to the opponents.

NEED FOR ARTIFICIAL BIDS

Yes, we prefer natural bidding, but unfortunately, natural bidding does not take care of all possible hands. It is only when the natural style won't suffice that it is prudent to adopt an artificial convention.

The Stayman Convention is especially necessary, for it covers situations left vague by natural bidding. In the introduction to this book, we stated: "In the old days, when one player opened one notrump and his partner bid two in a major suit, it was anybody's guess whether responder had a 4- or 5-card suit, whether his hand, overall, was anemic or robust." The Stayman Convention dispels this ambiguity.

Surely this is not the only situation that does not succumb to natural bidding; it is reasonable enough to employ a carefully thought-out convention to fill the gap.

We've often been asked, "Doesn't the Stayman two-club bid make it impossible to play a hand at two clubs?" Indeed it does. But if two clubs is a good spot for the hand, you probably won't be allowed to rest there. An experienced opponent will realize that if you are willing to settle for eight tricks, his side has enough tickets to compete, and it is comparatively easy to get into the auction when the bidding is about to subside at two clubs.

Since we are unlikely to play at two clubs, it is prudent to use the bid for a better purpose. In fact, in my favorite partnership, we go one step further: we give up all chance to play at two clubs when anyone at the table—ourselves, our partner or one of the opponents—bids one notrump. If you are interested in getting more mileage from your bidding, you might try this wrinkle with your favorite partner.

Here is a partial list of sequences where, under our system, two clubs has an artificial meaning, and shows interest in the majors:

	SOUTH		NORTH	
(1)	1♣ or 1◇		1♡ or 1♠	
	1NT		2♣	

	SOUTH		NORTH	
(2)	1♡		1♠	
	1NT		2♣	

	SOUTH	WEST	NORTH	
(3)	1♣ or 1◇	1NT	2♣	

	EAST	SOUTH	WEST	NORTH
(4)	1 of a suit	1NT	Pass	2♣

Sometimes *three* clubs is best played as an artificial asking bid, as in this sequence:

SOUTH	NORTH
1♣	1◇ or 1♡
2NT	3♣

South may have concealed a spade suit in order to make the more descriptive bid of two notrump. The three-club bid enables North to check back for a spade fit.

If the combined holdings were:

NORTH: ♠ K 9 7 3   ♡ Q J 10 6   ◇ 7 2   ♣ J 8 3
SOUTH: ♠ Q J 6 4   ♡ K 7   ◇ A 8 3   ♣ A K Q 4

South would now bid three spades and North would raise to four.

Most experienced partnerships would get to four spades via a different route:

SOUTH	NORTH
1♣	1♡
1♠	2♠
4♠	

That works fine on these hands, but what if North does not have four spades? For example:

NORTH: ♠ K 9 7   ♡ Q J 10 6   ◇ 7 3 2   ♣ J 8 3
SOUTH: ♠ Q J 6 4   ♡ K 7   ◇ A 8 3   ♣ A K Q 4

The bidding would probably go:

SOUTH	NORTH
1♣	1♡
1♠	1NT
3NT	Pass

Now the opponents have been warned away from leading either major suit. Against a diamond lead, you figure to lose three diamond tricks and the two major suit aces—down one. Moreover, the opening lead is more likely to be a diamond, rather than a club, since there are more diamonds (and more diamond honors) outstanding.

The trouble stems from the compulsion to show the spade suit. How much better to allow South the option to reveal or conceal the suit, and give North the tool to inquire, if he wishes. That is the advantage of using three clubs as an artificial asking bid in this sequence.

In this case, North doesn't use the bid, since he has only three spades himself:

SOUTH	NORTH
1♣	1♡
2NT	3NT

West may still come off to the killing opening, but he will have to find it all by himself.

DISADVANTAGES OF ARTIFICIAL BIDS

However, it is a waste of time to go out of your way to construct an artificiality when natural methods are adequate to the job. Most often the fault for a poor result lies with the player, not his method; a pet convention obscures, not solves, the problem.

Perhaps the chief disadvantages of any artificial bid is that it tends to delude the user into thinking he has been granted some magical advantage over other players. In truth, the very resort to a convention is a confession that the player could not cope with the situation by means of natural bidding methods. He may be even worse off trying to find his way through the morass of an artificial convention. *Another* method is not necessarily a *better* method. In fact a hastily contrived convention is a positive detriment to good bidding. A player cannot impulsively tamper with one troublesome situation without weakening the entire superstructure of his bidding. It is like the mad scientist who creates a monster only to find he cannot control it.

THE "FORGOTTEN" CONVENTION

Even experienced players forget conventions in the stress of combat. To cite one example, at one time we used two diamonds as an ace-asking bid, forcing to game, on a hand with a self-sufficient trump suit. Such a hand occurs so infrequently that it was almost inevitable that when the perfect situation did arise, our partner forgot we were using the convention and we arrived at a truly horrendous contract. Perhaps it is unnecessary to add that we discarded the convention on the spot. Yet we could well argue that it was a very simple and effective convention that covered a gap in natural bidding.

COUNTERMEASURES

For a while any new convention will show a profit, precisely because it is new and the opponents have not had an opportunity to develop a counter-weapon. But this is an unfair advantage, for the code of bridge ethics demands that your opponents know your special conventions *in advance,* so they can defend against them. They scarcely have the time—or inclination—to work out effective countermeasures for a complicated and esoteric convention with which they are unfamiliar. In effect then, you have given yourself an unfair advantage.

If your convention is really worth its salt, chances are other players will adopt it and still other players will develop defenses against it. The more the convention is used, the slimmer its advantage, for the defense tactics will keep pace with it.

A new convention is somewhat like the sensational rookie pitcher making his first appearance in baseball's major leagues: the second time around, he finds that the good hitters have solved his tricky deliveries.

VIRTUES OF NATURAL BIDDING

Natural bidding means that you bid what you have. If the bidding is sound, opponents will not get rich by doubling.

The natural bidding style also inhibits enemy action. Once you have struck the first blow with the opening bid, opponents may want to compete to find a suit fit of their own, but any seasoned player is reluctant to come into the bidding without a good suit or the strength that would otherwise warrant an opening bid. He is only too aware that if his hand does not strike a fit with partner's, he can be doubled and set badly.

THE BASIC FLAW OF ARTIFICIAL BIDS

The glaring weakness of any artificial bid stems from bidding a suit you do not have, for that is just the suit the opponents are most likely to have. They may have been afraid to risk an overcall, but they can now double your artificial bid to communicate the same message to partner without appreciable risk—particularly if the bid comes at a high level.

Once in a blue moon you or your partner will have length in the suit you bid artificially at a low level and can redouble to good effect. But most often an opponent will be able to double your artificial bid with impunity, thereby paving the way to a profitable save, directing the opening lead or indicating the best line of defense.

In short, there is a clear disadvantage to using any artificial bid, and you should satisfy yourself that the value of the bid outweighs this disadvantage.

The opening lead is often termed the "blind" lead; if your bidding system bathes it in the bright light of truth, you had better contract for a trick or two less than otherwise.

BASIC DEFENSE AGAINST ARTIFICIAL BIDS

From what we have said above, it naturally follows that a double of an artificial bid shows values in the artificially bid suit. In the sequence:

SOUTH	WEST	NORTH	EAST
1NT	Pass	2♣	Double
(strong)			

East's double shows a biddable club suit.*

---

* If North-South are playing weak notrump, East's double has a different meaning that has nothing to do with the club suit; it is a takeout double asking for West's better major suit. (This is covered in Chapter 13.) Note that this is an *exception* to the general rule that a double of an artificial bid shows length and strength in the suit bid.

Likewise in this sequence:

SOUTH	WEST	NORTH	EAST
1NT	Pass	2♣	Pass
2◇	Double		

West advertises a good diamond suit with his double. Note how this sequence illustrates the drawback of artificiality just mentioned: West is not strong enough to bid two diamonds on his own, following South's notrump opening, but the artificial bid allows him to show the suit anyway. If North later becomes declarer at a major-suit contract, East has a useful headstart in picking the opening lead and planning the defense.

Similarly in these auctions:

SOUTH	WEST
2♣	Double
(artificial)	

and

SOUTH	WEST	NORTH	EAST
2♣	Pass	2◇	Double
(artificial)		(artificial)	

the doubler shows length and strength in the suit bid to his right.

Technically, of course, these are all penalty doubles, but there is virtually no chance of their sticking. Still, it is a tasty treat to be able to double with one good suit and nothing else in the hand.

THREE CLUBS OVER TWO CLUBS

In the following auction, the meaning of North's bid is often misunderstood:

SOUTH	WEST	NORTH
1NT	2♣	3♣

Most players automatically assume that the three-club bid is a cue-bid, forcing to game. This is true *only* if West's bid is a natural bid, showing a genuine club suit. But you cannot cue-bid over an artificial bid. If West bid two clubs for takeout, then a three-club overcall has the same meaning as if West had remained silent—a desire to play at three clubs. This competitive action adds to the bidding arsenal. How else could you handle the hand cited on page 155?

♠ 6 ♡ Q 9 6 ◇ 8 5 2 ♣ Q 10 8 6 4 3

ARTIFICIALITY AD NAUSEAM

The superstructure of the Stayman Convention is solid. Over the years a wing or two has been added, and some needed reconstruction has been completed. But a number of well-intentioned architects would tamper with the very foundations. Several "modifications" have been proposed, and one is more artificial than the next. The weakness of all is that they call for the disclosure of hand pattern and strength that may be of no use to partner, but is a great comfort to the enemy. We shall examine the more common of these gadgets, expose their flaws and thus try to warn the reader away from them.

THREE CLUBS TO SHOW BOTH MAJORS

Some players stumble all over themselves to volunteer information about their major-suit holdings. We are often asked why opener cannot use one bid— three clubs—to show possession of both major suits after a two-club inquiry. Well, put yourself in the East seat after this auction:

SOUTH	NORTH
1NT	2♣
3♣*	4♠

It is your turn to make a "blind lead." Go back over the bidding and you will find it is not so blind after all. You know that South has four spades and four hearts; since his opening notrump advertised a balanced hand, his minor suits must be divided 3–2. This tidbit may be just the ticket to guide you to the killing opening lead. If it doesn't suffice, don't blame the opponents; they went all out to help you.

Now, assume your opponents are not using the three-club gimmick. The bidding would proceed:

SOUTH	NORTH
1NT	2♣
2♠	4♠

This time you are on lead in the West seat. What do you know about South's hand? Only that he has four spades. He might have five. In hearts, he could have two, three, four, even five cards. He might have four—or five—cards in one of the minors, or then again, he might not. Tote it all up and what have you got? Only the vaguest idea of South's distribution—certainly not enough to steer you to the killing lead. And all through the play you and your part-

---

* Shows 4-card holding in both major suits.

ner will have to work out declarer's hand pattern, because the bidding did not hand it to you on a silver platter.

ANOTHER DISADVANTAGE

An equally harmful effect of the wholesale answer is that the bidding gets too high too quickly. When you assign an overprecise meaning to each bid, it becomes impossible to stop in time at a reasonable part-score. A case in point—the bidding has gone:

SOUTH	NORTH
1NT	?

and you, North, hold:

> ♠ 9 7 6 2 ♡ 8 6 5 4 ◊ 8 7 6 5 2 ♣ None. What do you bid? Well, you would *like* to bid two clubs (Stayman) and pass partner's rebid. This should land you in a more playable contract than one notrump; either you will be in two of a major with a 4–4 fit or in two diamonds with the probability of a 5–3 fit.
>
> But you cannot bid two clubs if partner is allowed to respond three clubs. You certainly don't want to play this hand at the three level. Moreover, what do you bid over three clubs (or do you plan to pass!)? Whatever you bid, partner will take you to game if he has a maximum.*

TWO–NOTRUMP REBID TO SHOW A MAXIMUM

In the early days of Stayman, this was a commonplace auction:

SOUTH	NORTH
1NT	2♣
2NT	

---

* We do not wish to be unfair to the innovators who champion the three-club bid, and therefore point out that the usual version is that opener rebids three clubs with both majors and a *minimum* notrump, and three diamonds with both majors and a *maximum* notrump. In the sequence given, opener, who has shown a minimum notrump, will presumably pass partner's bid of three in a major suit. If the bidding has been

SOUTH	NORTH
1NT	2♣
3◊	

North can get out by passing, but look at the price he has paid: the hand has to be played at the three level and the known 4–4 fit has to be abandoned (actually two such major-suit fits are lost). If the three level is too high for this hand, the four level is grossly extravagant.

In a nutshell, you cannot handle weak three suiters that are short in clubs if you employ the three-club gimmick.

The two-notrump bid then showed the maximum notrump count with a hand lacking a 4-card major suit. It soon became apparent that this auction had the same drawback as the three-club rebid just reviewed—it is impossible for South to place the contract at two of the best combined suit.

Therefore this rebid has been discarded from the Stayman System. Rather than leave the bid completely idle, we have found one constructive use for it: the rare case of a maximum notrump with a doubleton diamond, a running club suit and no 4-card major. Here is an example:

♠ K 4 2 ♡ Q 7 5 ◇ J 3 ♣ A K Q J 5.

The principal gain in bidding two notrump on this type of hand is to avoid a two-diamond contract, when partner was planning to pass the conventional two-diamond response. No harm is done if partner intended to bid a 5-card major at the two level; responder knows that opener has a maximum notrump and 3-card support for his suit (he is marked with a doubleton diamond and would not have opened one notrump with a second doubleton), so responder can place the final contract at three or four of his major suit. It is interesting to observe that the two-notrump rebid does not really consume an extra round of bidding, as one might suppose. If the bidding had gone:

SOUTH	NORTH
1NT	2♣
2◇	2♡ (or 2♠)

South would surely make another bid in view of his maximum notrump and 3-card support.

TWO CLUBS FOR PART–SCORE— TWO DIAMONDS FOR GAME

Another variant is for responder to state his strength at the same time he inquires about his partner's major-suit holdings. Responder's bid of two clubs says he is looking for part-score only, while an immediate two-diamond call commits the partnership to game.

Here is the gadget in operation:

SOUTH	WEST	NORTH	EAST
1NT	Pass	2♣	?

You are sitting East, holding ♠ A 6 3 ♡ J 7 5 4 ◇ Q 10 9 7 6 ♣ 9. If you know that North's bid shows less than 8 points, you can scrape up a two-diamond butt-in bid without fear and trembling, for your partner is marked with at least 9 points. But if North's bid is unlimited in strength, it would be foolhardy for you to come into the auction.

This variant destroys the paralyzing effect of the Stayman two-club bid; in our opinion, it gains nothing, but gives up a great deal.

BIDDING TO SHOW WEAKNESS

The following is an advanced auction, previously discussed:

SOUTH	NORTH
1NT	2♣
2♦	3♣
3♠	

Opener's bid of three spades confirms a club fit and announces high cards in the spade suit. However, some innovators play the three-spade bid as showing *weakness* in the suit. Their theory is that since opener has only one weak suit, he should name it at this stage to describe his hand to the fullest. They point out—quite validly, we might add—that a bid in the strong suit tells nothing of the relative strength of the two remaining suits. This theory is very scientific and accurate as far as it goes. But it also ignores the salient fact that the opponents are listening. It is poor policy to play a system where the opponents know more than you want them to. Who knows but one opponent may double the "weakness bid" and his partner may have just enough in the suit to find a profitable save.

THE MORAL OF THE STORY

The first duty of the opener is to answer the question he was asked—no more or less. If partner wants to know more about a particular feature of your hand, he is perfectly capable of asking you to tell him more. Don't anticipate him! Wait until he asks!

♠ 15 THE SLAM HUNT

IT IS almost incomprehensible that there has never been an entire book devoted to slam bidding. The subject deserves one—perhaps a well-stocked library—for every day throughout America thousands of easy slams are missed. They represent a national waste, exceeded only by the thousands of impossible slams that are bid. Why Vance Packard did not deal with this vital subject in his book *The Waste Makers* remains a mystery to us.

AN AMERICAN HERITAGE

By all rights, Americans should be superb slam bidders. When an American, Harold S. Vanderbilt, invented contract bridge, he remembered that his countrymen like to "shoot the works" or "go for broke." So he introduced the slam feature which held out tempting bonuses for successful adventures. This element, as much as any other, added excitement to the game and led to its fantastic popular acceptance.

Another American bridge pioneer, Ely Culbertson, gave Americans *asking bids,* a somewhat controversial tool for locating key controls. In one form or another, they are used throughout the world, but rarely in America. Certainly Americans like to bid and make slams as much as anyone. But apparently they have always liked a free-wheeling, "go-as-you-please" approach instead of the intricacies of Mr. Culbertson's brainchild.

Is it fair to fault the average bridge player, who plays "for fun" and "can't bother to remember all those fancy conventions?" Perhaps not, but isn't it "more fun" to win? Accurate slam bidding goes a long way toward making a winner out of a mere card pusher.

But there can be little excuse for sloppy slam bidding at the expert level. It has been years since America won an international championship, and in most of those long years, the victor has shown himself decidedly more proficient in the slam department than we. Perhaps it is going too far to attribute our record of losses to this one factor, but it certainly has been a major contributing one.

THE EASY SLAMS

Fortunately we excel at some slams—particularly the ones that depend solely on the sheer mass of high cards. We are so point-count happy that we delight in adding our points to those of partner's and—eureka—"We have 33 points, ergo a slam!"

We have no desire to belittle these slams; they count just as much as the slams that must be ferreted out. But we *do* wish to emphasize that there are other kinds of slams—slams that depend upon suit fit and key control cards—and that these slams can be bid.

Before learning how to get to these tougher slams, it would be well to review the arithmetic and simple rules for bidding slams on sheer power. And to do so in expert fashion, we now have to consider a modern refinement that alters our computations.

WEAK AND INTERMEDIATE TWO-BIDS

Many players today use "weak two-bids." Under this convention, first developed by Howard Schenken, with whom we won three World's Championships, an opening bid of two diamonds, two hearts or two spades is not a strong bid at all, but rather a pre-emptive tactic. It describes a hand with (1) a good 6-card suit (no more than two losers), (2) strength in the 6-to-12-point range and (3) some outside defensive value—an ace or king.

Other players have adopted "intermediate two-bids," whereby the same three bids show big hands that are not quite strong enough to force to game.

Under both systems, two clubs becomes the sole game force. It is artificial; opener shows his independent suit at his second turn. But if he has a strong balanced hand and no independent suit, his natural rebid would be in notrump. Thus, this convention adds two new sequences to our notrump structure—an opening bid of two clubs followed by a minimum bid in notrump and the same opening two-club bid followed by a jump in notrump.

With these two new bidding tools, opener can define his hand within narrower limits than heretofore. Just as responder has a two-step sequence available to him, so has opener. And the same rule applies—that the two-step message shows a stronger hand than the immediate bid at the same level. Thus two clubs followed by a two-notrump bid is a bigger bid than an opening two-notrump call. The revised scale is as follows:

2NT	— 20-22 points
2♣, then 2NT	— 23-24 points
3NT	— 25-26 points
2♣, then 3NT	— 27-28 points

Forget about the scale of responses to invite slam on balanced hands; this is just an exercise in arithmetic anyway. It only helps in the remote case when both partners have 4–3–3–3 hand patterns. If *either* has any distributional feature, he should go slowly to ferret out a suit fit.

RECIPE FOR A SLAM

Successful slams have two elements: (1) declarer must be able to develop twelve tricks, but (2) he must cash them *before* the defenders can take two of their own. Totting up to 33 points does not make a slam; it merely guards against the defenders having two tricks off the top. Slams do not live on points alone, for points only measure high cards. Almost invariably declarer must promote small cards to winning rank in order to score his slam.

And that is where *fit* comes in. Unless you hold a self-sufficient suit, you will need help from your partner to develop winners out of your small cards. Take this extreme illustration: Would you want to be in a slam, *regardless of partner's holding*, with this hand?

♠ A K Q 7 6 5 2 ♡ A K ◇ A K ♣ K Q

The correct answer is *no*—not if partner is void in spades. If partner has as much as a single spade, the odds favor a 3–2 break, so that you can bring in the suit without loss. But if partner is void in spades, you need a 3–3 division, which is against the odds.

WHAT IS A SATISFACTORY FIT?

In the preceding case, a 7–1 spade distribution suffices for your cause, while 7–0 does not. Most of the time you'll be looking at 4-, 5- and, occasionally, 6-card suits. Whenever the percentages favor opposing distribution that prevents the loss of a trick you cannot afford, you have a satisfactory fit. Otherwise the element of fit is lacking.

This element of fit, like the law of gravity, is always present whether or not we are aware of it. Even the easy-to-bid "sheer power" slams we have been discussing require a minimum fit. Remember these so-called "point-count" slams stem from an opening notrump bid, which assures partner of a balanced distribution. Thus responder knows he will find at least a doubleton—and probably three cards—in support of his long suit. Conversely, if responder's hand is also balanced, the odds favor one or more 4–4 or 4–3 suit fits.

SLAMS ON LESS THAN 33 POINTS!

The last hand contained 28 high-card points, yet provided a fine play for slam opposite any Yarborough that includes a singleton spade.

Many other slams can be made with less than 33 high-card points, as long as the hands fit well. When your singleton or void is in the same suit as partner's small cards—when you have a set-up side suit—when your honor cards help solidify partner's suit—when a 4–4 trump fit is disclosed (so that either hand can develop an additional ruffing trick)—in all these cases you know the hands fit well.

About the only time you need 33 high-card points for slam is when you cannot discover whether the hands fit each other.

Even with 33 points assured, it may pay to take a second look. What do you do with this hand after your partner opens one notrump?

♠ A 7   ♡ K J 2   ♢ A Q 6 4   ♣ A 8 4 3

Most players would bid six notrump on this reasoning: "I have a balanced hand, and my 18 points added to partner's 15 give us 33, enough for small slam; there is no chance for a grand slam, so I'll save time by bidding six notrump myself." Or, if they know their responses, they will bid five notrump, which amounts to about the same thing.

But what if this happens to be the layout:

NORTH: ♠ A 7   ♡ K J 2   ♢ A Q 6 4   ♣ A 8 4 3
SOUTH: ♠ K J 6 3   ♡ A 7   ♢ K J 8 2   ♣ Q J 6

Oh, six notrump may come home all right. All declarer needs is for *both* major-suit finesses to work. Or a favorable club lie—either a 3–3 break or the king with East so a backward finesse will work—and then he needs only one successful finesse in the majors. But *which* major suit? Declarer has to guess right the first time; he won't get a second chance.

But at a diamond slam, declarer gets *three* chances: a favorable club lie *or* ruffing out the queen of spades; if neither works, he can fall back on the heart finesse. All told, he has about a 68 percent chance plus other possibilities if he is adroit at squeeze play. But six notrump makes only about 41 percent of the time.

If North recognizes the importance of 4–4 trump fit and the value of the extra ruffing trick it delivers, he will go more slowly. Here is how the slam can be reached:

SOUTH	NORTH
1NT	2♣ (a)
2♠	3◇ (b)
3NT (c)	5NT (d)
6◇ (e)	

(a) Not really interested in the majors, but the Stayman bid sets the stage for asking about the diamond suit.
(b) As planned.
(c) Despite the fine fit for diamonds, holding a minimum notrump, South can do no more than bid three notrump.
(d) "I want to be in slam; pick your spot."
(e) "In that case, I like diamonds."

Here 33 points yield a subpar play for a notrump slam; yet slam in the 4–4 trump suit is odds-on. When you are not sure the partnership assets total 33 points, the case for fit exploration becomes stronger. In fact, the more fit, the fewer points you need.

Let's follow another well-bid slam:

NORTH:	♠ A 8 6 4	♡ Q 7	◇ K 10 6 5	♣ A K 10
SOUTH:	♠ K 5 3	♡ A K 6	◇ A Q 9 4	♣ 7 5 3

SOUTH	NORTH
1NT	2♣ (a)
2◇	3◇ (b)
3♡ (c)	3♠ (d)
4◇ (e)	6◇ (f)

(a) North could bid four notrump to show his point count, but that leads to slam only when South has a maximum 17 points. Even then, notrump may not be the best spot. A trump fit is usually worth an extra trick, so North correctly explores the spade suit first.

(b) No luck in spades; maybe diamonds will be luckier.

(c) "You found me; I have a good four-card diamond fit, as well as heart strength and better than a minimum notrump." At this point, North could bid six diamonds without further ado, since there are too many holes for a grand slam. But let's follow the rest of the auction through, for it is a valuable exercise in the techniques of slam bidding:

(d) Both a slam try and a cue-bid showing the ace of spades. If North were not slam-minded, he would rebid four diamonds or three notrump. And South can be sure North has the spade ace, for once the trump suit is set, the first cue-bid in any side suit shows the ace of that side suit. (Before a trump fit is established, a cue-bid in a side suit may show a high-card combination, such as K Q, K J—or even just king, if no better bid is available—but not necessarily the ace.)

(e) South has several bids available to him. He chooses to return to the agreed suit, for it is the most innocuous and least encouraging. South is wary of slam, for the partnership has talked over every suit but clubs and South cannot help out in that department. If he had the club ace, he would cue-bid it now. If he had sure second-round club control, he could jump to six diamonds himself. If he had K x in clubs, he would bid five notrump, which says, "I have second-round control of the fourth suit—clubs—but it's not a sure stopper, so I don't want the opening lead to come through me. How about playing the hand from my side—in six notrump—so they can't lead through me?"

Summing up, South has four bids to describe his holding in the fourth suit: (1) returning to the agreed suit, diamonds, as the lowest level, to confess he has no high card in the suit; (2) cue-bidding clubs to show the ace, (3) jumping to slam in the agreed suit, diamonds, to show sure second-round club control (K Q in this case, but if South were not marked with a balanced hand and therefore at least a doubleton club, it could equally be based on a singleton); and (4) a bid of five notrump to show the guarded king.

South might also bid four spades. This would show the king of spades, since the second cue-bid in a side suit shows second-round control. However, this sounds encouraging, since it volunteers more information. Note though that it does not take the partner past the agreed game level—five diamonds—so it does not commit the partnership to slam.

(f) North has the clubs well under control, so the only question is whether to go for a small or grand slam. Each of the four suits has a potential loser and South cannot be expected to fill all the gaps. Therefore North wisely decides to settle for a small slam. Technically he could cue-bid six clubs to show the ace of that suit. But the theory of cue-bidding is that you give information only when you are unsure of the final contract. A cue-bid at the six level after the trump suit has been decided therefore inquires about a grand slam. North is not quite strong enough for this aggressive move. If he had an extra queen somewhere, the cue-bid would be in order.

SECRETS OF SLAM BIDDING

This sequence illustrates several facets of slam bidding:

1. Use of the Stayman two-club bid to find out about suit fits—both the majors and the minors.

2. The *implied* fit: a bid that cannot logically show a real suit implies a fit with the suit just bid by partner. At the same time it indicates a high card in the suit actually bid.

3. Cue-bidding after a trump suit has been agreed upon. The first time a side suit is bid shows first-round control (ace or void); the second time, second-round control (king or singleton). A cue-bid implies uncertainty about how high to bid (otherwise why mess around?) and therefore asks partner to help in making the decision.

4. Identification of the key suit: When the trump suit has been set and two side suits have been cue-bid, both partners are alerted to the danger of the fourth suit. If one partner cannot stop that suit, he returns to the agreed trump suit at the lowest level and the slam hunt is abandoned unless the other has second-round control. With first-round control, he cue-bids the suit; with a sure second-round stopper, he bids six in the agreed trump suit. If the player who bid notrump first holds the guarded king, he bids five notrump to avoid an opening lead through that suit. Here is a further refinement of this principle, which also illustrates another facet of slam bidding:

NORTH: ♠ A Q 9 4 ♡ K 5 ◇ K J 7 6 4 ♣ Q 8
SOUTH: ♠ K 8 6 3 ♡ A 9 7 ◇ A Q 8 ♣ K 7 2

SOUTH	NORTH
1NT	2♣
2♠	3◇ (a)
3NT (b)	4♠ (c)
5♡ (d)	5♠ (e)
5NT (f)	6♠ (g)

(a)   North could take a chance and leap to six spades at this point. But there may be two quick club tricks off the hand. Since he doesn't know how well the hands fit, he explores a bit further and tells about his diamond values on the way.

(b) A forced response, since South has neither four hearts nor four diamonds. (If this isn't completely clear, better reread p. 101.)

(c) South's last bid helped not at all, so North bids the game where he knows it belongs.

(d) Now it is revealed that the three-diamond bid was really a mild slam try, for if North were only interested in game, he would have bid four spades at his second turn. South is only too happy to co-operate in the slam hunt, as he has excellent diamond support and almost all his values are in aces and kings, where they should be most useful.

(e) North can do no more, for clubs are still wide open as far as he knows.

(f) South shows the guarded club king, and suggests a notrump slam played from his side.

(g) North knows a lead through partner's king cannot cost his side two quick club tricks, for his own queen provides sure second-round control. So he bids the slam in the agreed suit. If North lacked the club queen, and had, say, the heart queen instead, he might follow partner's lead and bid six notrump, which has the same chance of success as the actual six-spade contract—a 3–2 spade break, odds of 62 percent in his favor.

Theoretically North could pass five notrump, if he suddenly got cold feet. But it is a capital bridge crime to go past game, stop short of slam and end up in the wrong denomination to boot.

OTHER BRIDGE CRIMES

Experienced bridge players have an aversion to certain contracts, viz., three or five in a major suit or four notrump. There is no advantage in contracting for one trick more than necessary; you feel downright sheepish when you go down a trick at such a contract, for you could have chalked up a plus score just by stopping one level lower. Down one at three of a major is only a misdemeanor in the bridge code of justice, for all it throws away is a part-score. But down one at four notrump or five of a major is a felony: it tosses away a game for no apparent compensating advantage. By these standards stopping at five no-trump on the previous hand and going down one is a hanging offense, for the culprit took two shots to kick away the game.

"DON'T GET PAST GAME!"

That is why knowledgeable bridge players hesitate to get past the game level. Yet most are unduly timid. All through this chapter we champion the cause of exploring for slam *below* the game level. But there are times when it is impossible to look for slam intelligently without getting up to the five level.

If you know the hands fit well and include an extra margin of strength beyond what is needed for game, you should not be afraid to go a level higher in search of slam. Usually you will be safe enough at the higher level. If you are set once in thirty times, it is worth it, for you'll probably bid at least four successful slams as a result of your daring. If you are never guilty of the crime of being set at five of a major suit, then you are not trying hard enough for the enticing slam bonus. The purpose of any intelligent bidding system is to land you in reasonable contracts, not ironclad ones. Even reasonable contracts go down when the percentages turn fickle. But to get to a reasonable contract, you must occasionally stumble along the way and arrive at an impossible one. There isn't a bridge "great" who hasn't fallen, even as the veriest hack. Console thyself and bid those slams!

START BELOW THE GAME LEVEL

But most slam tries can be made below the game level. It is fortunate that this is so, for few players can be prodded beyond game unless the Bank of England has underwritten a slam.

The road to slam should be smoother after an opening one-notrump bid, for this is the most descriptive and precise bid of all; it permits scales of responses that accurately delineate the partnership holdings, with clear demarcation between weak, strong and forcing bids. But, alas, notrump is also the shortest road to *game* and it is a prodigous feat to budge a partner off this familiar highway. It has taken years to persuade the average bridge player to move out of notrump into superior game contracts at a suit. As for *slams,* whew! If he doesn't smell a notrump slam right off, wild horses won't budge him past three notrump.

DIAGNOSING SLAMS

And yet, oddly enough, the reason most often given for *not* making a slam try is the fear of getting partner "all excited" and driving him headlong into some wildly impossible contract. How preposterous! A slam try is nothing more than a *tentative* slam *suggestion.* It doesn't *promise* a slam. It doesn't even indicate a slam is *likely;* it just states that a slam is *possible.*

A "slam try" says, "Partner, we are already committed to game, but there is just a chance our hands might fit well enough for slam. Therefore, as a start, I want to tell you about this particular feature of my hand, which might prove valuable in a slam effort. Obviously, if I'm even whispering about slam possibilities, I think game is odds-on, so I have full values—perhaps a shade more—for my bidding so far. But we don't want to throw away an odds-on game for some slim hope of slam, do we? So don't get the idea that I am *insisting* on slam. If I have substantial values above what I have shown, you will hear from me again. In the meantime, if you have a feature that you think will help us in slam, tell me about it. Let's keep telling each other about these features—below the game level—until one of us has enough information to bid the slam or, in the absence of that information, we settle for game by default. If you have stretched your hand already or have no slam feature to pass on, just return to our agreed suit or to notrump, if that looks better. Remember, I am not forcing you to slam, only making a mild suggestion."

A slam has to start somewhere; someone must make the first move. But that first move is not a command. There may be as many as five separate bits of information that have to be fitted together before a slam can be bid intelligently. Think of tries as a series of entries on a checklist; as soon as either partner sees that all the necessary items have been checked off, he bids the slam. If neither partner can complete the checklist, then only game is bid. It is a cooperative effort, for each partner has elements to contribute to a slam.

DON'T BE AFRAID TO LOOK

The first step in bidding a slam is the recognition that it is barely possible. Think back to the last time you were in four of a major, making two overtricks, and you and your partner solemnly agreed that it was "just lucky; sure the hands fitted perfectly, but there was no way we could find out." Wasn't there? Didn't either of you pause for a split second during the bidding, thinking, "If partner has thus-and-so, we . . . oh, but it is just too unlikely."

Ah, but there's the rub! It is not *your* role to decide what partner's hand is. If there is a chance for slam, describe what *you* can offer toward it, and let your partner tell about *his* hand. Giving partner room can add thousands of points to your score.

Here is an excellent slam that was reached because each partner allowed for the possibility and gave the other leeway:

NORTH: ♠ 7 5 4   ♡ J 8 6 5 3 2   ◇ A 4   ♣ 9 3
SOUTH: ♠ A 6   ♡ A K 7 4   ◇ K Q 3   ♣ A K 8 4

SOUTH	NORTH
2♣	2◇ (a)
2NT (b)	3♡ (c)
3♠ (d)	4◇ (e)
5♣ (f)	5♡ (g)
6◇ (h)	6♡ (i)
Pass (j)	

(a)   Conventional negative response to an artificial two-club forcing bid.

(b)   Showing 23-24 points.

(c)   Four hearts is the "book bid," but what's the hurry? North can always bid four hearts over a three-notrump rebid. South might just have a maximum hand, good heart fit, lots of key control cards, and he may relish the chance to show that by bidding a new suit along the way. Give him room.

(d)   Sure enough, South has just that kind of hand, and his bid shows a high spade honor, maximum notrump and excellent heart support.

(e)   Showing the ace of diamonds, the one feature North can contribute to a slam venture. Note that the bidding is still below the game level.

(f)   That's all South needs to bid six; he can count one spade, five hearts, three diamonds, two clubs and a probable ruff. But there might be a biddable grand slam, so South continues by cue-bidding the ace of clubs.

(g)   Nothing more to show.

(h)   South makes one last try by cue-bidding second-round control of diamonds.

(i)   Still can't offer anything more than he has done.

(j)   Abiding by his partner's decision.

To be sure, this is a delicate and expert sequence of bids, but the slam is biddable. However, if North bids four hearts at his first turn, South is forced to pass and the post-mortem comment will be the usual "Lucky hand; fits perfectly, but there was no way we could bid it."

South cannot budge over a four-heart rebid; to do so would be a bridge crime of the first order—and a breach of partnership faith. Besides, for all he knows, North might have the following hand for his four-heart bid:

♠ 52 ♡ Q J 9 8 6 3 ◇ 6 5 2 ♣ 7 2

and an exploratory bid past four hearts could put the pair overboard.

THE INDIRECT RAISE

Earlier we observed that the partners must first agree on a trump suit before either can cue-bid an ace. Agreement on a trump suit ordinarily comes about when one partner raises the other's suit. But it is also wise to conduct slam inquiries below the game level, and a raise in a suit consumes a vital level of bidding and may land the pair right at game level. This apparent contradiction is often resolved by an indirect raise which implies a fit. This does three things at once: (1) it confirms the trump suit, (2) it shows a high value in the suit actually bid and (3) it conserves a level of bidding. It is probably the most valuable slam-bidding tool in our kit. Rather than abandon it, we would surrender the overused Blackwood Convention.

Because of the importance of the indirect raise, we shall dwell on it a bit longer. First, contrast these two auctions:

	SOUTH	NORTH
(1)	1NT	3♡
	3♠	
(2)	1NT	3♡
	4♡	

In (1) South confirms the heart fit, a maximum notrump and a spade honor, all at the same time. This leaves room for North to bid four diamonds to indicate a high value there—and the hand is still below the game level. It is theoretically possible for South to return to four hearts and for North to pass him there. For example, if the hands were:

NORTH: ♠ K 5   ♡ K J 8 7 3   ◇ A J 10 5   ♣ 9 2
SOUTH: ♠ A J 3   ♡ A Q 9   ◇ K Q 7 4 2   ♣ 10 3

the bidding would go:

SOUTH	NORTH
1NT	3♡
3♠	4◇
4♡	Pass

With two quick club losers, South doesn't want to venture past the game level. North too has two quick losers in clubs, so he passes four hearts.

But while this sequence is safe and the bidding can subside at game, it can also lead to an excellent slam:

NORTH: ♠ 6 5   ♡ K J 8 7 3   ◇ A 9 2   ♣ K 6 4
SOUTH: ♠ A 8 3   ♡ A Q 9   ◇ 10 3   ♣ A Q 7 4 2

SOUTH	NORTH
1NT	3♡
3♠	4◇
5♣	6♡

This time South has the club ace to cue-bid and North carries on to slam. North's last bid may seem on the aggressive side, but South's cue-bid promotes the value of his own club king and all his cards appear well placed.

RECOGNIZING AN INDIRECT RAISE

If the concept of the indirect raise is a new one to you, you are probably asking yourself, "How can I tell when my partner is giving me an indirect raise and when he is showing me a real suit?" If the flavor of the auction indicates that opener may be bidding a real suit, then by all means assume he has made a natural bid.

But the bidding structure after an opening notrump bid makes responder the captain and opener is supposed to answer responder's inquiries, not trot out new suits just to liven up the bidding. Thus if opener volunteers information about a suit—rather than replying to a question—then he is giving an indirect raise.

Frequently his bidding wouldn't make sense under any other interpretation:

SOUTH	NORTH
1NT	2♣
2♢	2♡
2♠	

South denied holding four spades, so his belated spade bid must indicate a high spade honor and an indirect heart raise with a maximum hand. Why else bid a suit that cannot possibly become trump? It would be an impossible bid. Every bid must have a meaning and we get more mileage out of our bidding structure by using a "wasted" bid that would otherwise lie fallow.

SNIFFING OUT A SLAM

Slam bidding is more of an art than a science; it demands imagination more than pat techniques. But it is one of the greatest thrills in bridge to gradually smoke out a slam, bid it and then bring it home with good play.

But you have to be on the lookout to find these prizes. The more unbalanced your hand, the more your fancy should turn to thoughts of slam. Unbalanced hands become veritable powerhouses when opener's controls are in the right places, and you'll never know unless you ask. In Chapter 11 we saw how the concept of the "three-suit deck" paves the way to some truly artistic slams. Cue-bidding aces after a trump suit has been set helps in the same way.

ACE-COUNTING CONVENTIONS

Still, some slams depend less upon the location than the number of aces in partner's hand, so we should touch on the ace-counting conventions that cope with them. Unfortunately these conventions also create problems of their own.

Every bridge player is only too familiar with—and often even enamored of—the Blackwood four-notrump convention which asks partner to tell how many aces he holds. There is nothing wrong with the convention, but too many players use it as their only slam-bidding device, ignoring the far more useful cue-bidding, shape-showing and indirect raise techniques. Furthermore, they are not really sure when a four-notrump bid is Blackwood and when it is a natural notrump raise—a general directional slam try. This confusion can be eliminated if the Gerber ace-asking convention is integrated into your bidding system.

THE GERBER CONVENTION

The Gerber Convention employs four clubs as the jumping-off point for counting aces. It was invented by John Gerber as a substitute for Blackwood in order to start the inquiry at a lower level. A follow-up bid of five clubs asks for kings. (This is a widely accepted variation from Gerber's original method.)

Gradually experts have come to rely on Gerber as the primary tool after an opening bid in notrump while retaining Blackwood as the asking bid after an opening in a suit. Still there is some confusion as to when four clubs or four notrump is conventional, and when it is natural.

A CLEAR-CUT DISTINCTION

We go one step further to avoid any possible ambiguity. We use Gerber as the primary ace-asking convention when the auction starts with notrump. If the bidding sequence leaves room for a four-club call and a player elects to bid four notrump instead, then he is giving a natural notrump raise. But if the four-club bid is not available, a four-notrump bid is Blackwood.

See how well this works in the following situations that would otherwise be ambiguous:

	SOUTH	NORTH	
(1)	1NT	3♠	Blackwood—no room for Gerber.
	4♠	4NT	
(2)	1NT	3♠	A notrump raise, not Blackwood; four clubs,
	3NT	4NT	Gerber, is available to ask for aces.

That still leaves the problem of when four clubs is Gerber and when it is a cue-bid. There is no fully satisfactory rule we've been able to find, so we play every four-club bid as Gerber when the bidding has started with one notrump. The theory is that it cannot *hurt* to know how many aces partner has and it might *help*. In any event, this approach dispels all ambiguity and puts the partnership at ease.

ROMAN RESPONSES

Many American players have adopted the Italian refinement of identifying the aces when responder holds exactly two. In this auction:

SOUTH	NORTH
1NT	3♡
4♡	4NT

a five-club response shows zero or three aces, five diamonds shows one or four aces, five hearts shows two "like" aces (both majors, both minors, both red suits or both black suits), five spades shows two "unlike aces." If North holds one ace and hears a five-heart reply, he can identify one of South's aces. For example, if North has the club ace, he can rule out South's holding both minor aces and both black aces. So South holds aces in both majors or both red suits. He is therefore sure to hold the heart ace. A short-cut to remember this is the "double opposite": partner holds the ace of the opposite color and the opposite rank; when you hold a black minor ace (clubs), partner has the red major ace (hearts).

If South replies five spades to four notrump, to show two unlike aces, North can positively identify partner's two aces. Since he himself holds the club ace, North knows his partner holds the diamond and spade aces (and lacks the "double opposite" ace).

MODIFIED ROMAN

We used the Roman responses for a while and never found a case where identification of the aces was crucial. But twice the response guided the defense to the right opening lead. Therefore we have since discarded Roman "like-unlike" responses for aces. The way we play it, a five-heart response to Blackwood shows two aces but does not identify which (we retain five clubs to show zero or three aces, and five diamonds to show one or four, for this adjustment allows us to stop at a five-heart contract when two aces are missing). We follow the same formula for Gerber. If it is urgent to know which ace partner holds, we try to steer the bidding so that he will cue-bid it.

Kings are a different matter. When your side has all four aces, knowledge of which kings partner holds often enables you to bid a playable grand slam or stay out of an inferior one.

Therefore we use our own modified Roman responses to identify the kings, both for Blackwood and Gerber. Here is a Gerber auction:

SOUTH	NORTH
INT	3♠
3NT	4♣
4◊ , 4♡ or 4♠	5♣

North's bid asks about kings. The responses are:

SOUTH'S BID OVER GERBER FIVE CLUBS	NUMBER OF KINGS SOUTH HOLDS
5◊	0 or 3 (with at least 1 in unbid suit)
5♡	1 (in unbid suit) or 4
5♠	1 (in bid suit)
5NT	2 (at least 1 in unbid suit)
6♣	2 (both in bid suits)
6◊	3 (all in bid suits)

By "bid suit" we mean one that was bid naturally. An opening artificial two-club or a Stayman two-club response therefore does not qualify.

THE TRUMP SUIT

Nobody has come up with a means of cue-bidding in the agreed trump suit. The cheapest bid in the trump suit is generally used as a noncommittal bid to indicate no side-suit value to cue-bid or else a lack of enthusiasm about slam prospects. Even a jump in the trump suit does not show anything about the quality of that suit, but rather indicates general slam bullishness and no available cue-bid. Therefore you have to elicit data on the trump suit indirectly:

SOUTH	NORTH
1NT	3♡
3♠	4◊
5♣	5♡

North holds:

♠ K Q 5 ♡ J 8 6 5 4 2 ◊ A 10 ♣ K 9

South's three-spade bid sets hearts as trump by inference. North suggests a slam, and the partnership cue-bids the three side aces. Yet North fails to bid the slam. Obviously, he is concerned about trump solidity.

Here are two possible hands South might hold:

(1)   ♠ A J   ♡ Q 9 7 3   ◊ K Q 8 6   ♣ A 8 6
(2)   ♠ A 8   ♡ K Q 9 7   ◊ K 8 6 4   ♣ A 8 6

South would pass with (1), since his hearts are anything but robust. But with (2)—holding two of the top three hearts—he would bid a slam in hearts.

THE GRAND SLAM FORCE

If North held this hand: ♠ K Q 7 ♡ A 8 6 5 4 2 ◊ A 10 ♣ K 9, the bidding would evolve differently:

SOUTH	NORTH
1NT	3♡
3♠	4◊
5♣	5NT
6♡ or 7♡	Pass

Once South shows the club ace, North thinks about a grand slam. North uses the grand-slam force—a bid of five notrump—to ask South to bid a grand slam with two of the top three trump honors, but to stop at six with any lesser trump holding. Thus with (1) above South bids six hearts, but with (2), he bids seven.

This convention works fine, but it comes up rarely and is oriented only to grand slams. If somebody invents a workable "small-slam force" it should entitle him to a niche in bridge's Hall of Fame.

Note that not every five-notrump bid is a grand-slam force. It can be the follow-up to Blackwood, viz.:

SOUTH	NORTH
1NT	2♣
2♠	3♡
4♡	4NT
5♡	5NT

or a quantitative bid:

SOUTH	NORTH
1NT	2♣
2◊	5NT

and there is a third possibility. How would you interpret the five-notrump bid in this sequence?

SOUTH	NORTH
1♣	1♡
2♣	3♡
3NT	5NT

North's five notrump asks South to pick the spot to play the slam—hearts or notrump or even one of the black suits if South has a near-solid 5-card suit. North might have this hand:

♠ K 6 ♡ A Q 8 7 5 2 ◊ Q 9 5 ♣ K 2

Consider the logic: no trump suit has been set, so North cannot cue-bid a side ace even if he had one. For the same reason, he cannot bid Gerber (or Blackwood) asking for aces. He doesn't want to bid his hearts yet a third time and he can't support either of partner's suits since he has only a doubleton in each. There are enough high cards and fit for slam, but where to play it? The five-notrump bid asks South to pick the spot. With something like K x or J x in hearts, South would bid six hearts; with A Q J x x in a black suit, he should bid the slam there. Otherwise six notrump is probably best.

GRAND SLAM FORCE AFTER BLACKWOOD

Occasionally in bridge you have a chance to eat your cake and have it too. We have found a way to use the grand-slam force even after Blackwood:

SOUTH	NORTH
1♡	3♡
4NT	5◊
6♣ or 6◊	

The bid of a new suit at the six level after Blackwood is a wasted bid so we developed a way to use it advantageously. It asks partner to bid seven hearts (the agreed suit) if he has two of the top three heart honors. Of course, in the process South assures his partner that all four aces are held. Note too that South's bid at the six level must be below the rank of the agreed suit.

Do not confuse this auction with the following one:

SOUTH	NORTH
1♣	3♣
4NT	5◊
5♡ or 5♠	

A new suit at the *five* level after Blackwood asks partner to bid five notrump, for there is a shortage of aces for slam and it is too late to play at five of the agreed suit.

South may have room to return to five of the agreed suit and prefer a notrump contract nonetheless:

SOUTH	NORTH
1♢	1♡
3♡	4♢
4NT	5♢
5♠	

Apparently South fears an opening lead through a guarded king in a side suit, if he returns to hearts. So he asks partner to bid five notrump so South can play the hand from his side of the table.

L'ENVOI

Bridge is more fun when you use your thinking cells rather than your memory cells. We hope this book helps you enjoy the game more and that you will invest part of your new-found winnings in a book for one of the losers in your game.

SUMMARY—

MEANING OF BIDS

(PART II)

THE FOLLOWING PAGES recap the meanings of bids and bidding sequences covered in Part II for the advanced player. It is hoped that these pages will help as a handy checklist and refresher.

The explanation applies to the last bid in the sequence, which is underlined. It takes into account the previous auction. Unless otherwise noted, the opponents have not entered into the bidding, nor has partner passed.

The methods recommended for advanced players in Part II are built upon the superstructure for the average player, as outlined in Part I. Many of the sequences retain their meaning. In order to concentrate on what is new and different and to avoid repetition, the Part I sequences are not repeated in this summary.

1. OPENING BID OF ONE NOTRUMP

A. *When vulnerable:*

OPENER
1NT

"Strong" notrump, 15–17 points, stoppers in three suits, balanced hand (may be 5–4–2–2 if doubletons are as good as A Q, or 6–3–2–2 with near-solid minor and two strong doubletons). No 5-card major as good as K J x x x.

B.   When not vulnerable:

OPENER
1NT

"Weak" notrump, 12–14 points, balanced shape, high cards in three suits, no 5-card major as good as K J x x x.

2. STAYMAN CONVENTION
A.   Basic adjustment:

	SOUTH	NORTH
(1)	1NT	*2♣*

Stayman Convention, asks partner to name a biddable 4-card major suit. *North does not promise a 4-card major of his own.*

	SOUTH	NORTH
(2)	1NT	2♣
	2♠	*3NT*

South must pass, for North does not have four hearts.

	SOUTH	NORTH
(3)	1NT	2♣
	2♠	*2NT*

No statement about the heart suit. Therefore South cannot bid three hearts unless he has a maximum notrump in addition to a biddable 4-card heart suit. He is barred from bidding four hearts.

	SOUTH	NORTH
(4)	1NT	2♣
	2♠	2NT
	3♡	

Maximum notrump and 4-card heart suit.

	SOUTH	NORTH
(5)	1NT	2♣
	2♠	2NT
	Pass	

Minimum-range notrump, could have four hearts.

	SOUTH	NORTH
(6)	1NT	2♣
	2◊ , 2♡	*3♣ or 3◊*
	or 2♠	

Strength in the suit bid, asks South for more information, game force.

	SOUTH	NORTH
(7)	1NT	2♣
	2♠	3♣ or 3◊
	3♡	

Biddable 4-card heart suit, may be maximum or miminum, game force already exists.

	SOUTH	NORTH
(8)	1NT	2♣
	2♠	3♣
	3◇	

No biddable 4-card heart suit, good 4-card fit in clubs (approximately Q J x x or better), high diamond honor combination, better than a minimum notrump.

	SOUTH	NORTH
(9)	1NT	2♣
	2♠	3♣
	4♣	

No biddable 4-card heart suit, good 4-card club fit, maximum notrump, wariness about at least one red suit for notrump.

	SOUTH	NORTH
(10)	1NT	2♣
	2♠	3♣
	3NT	

No biddable 4-card heart suit, no good 4-card club fit, hence preference for notrump on evenly balanced hand.

	SOUTH	NORTH
(11)	1NT	2♣
	2♠	3♣
	3♠	

No biddable 4-card heart suit, 5-card spade suit weaker than K J x x x.

	SOUTH	NORTH
(12)	1NT	2♣
	2◇	3◇
	3♡ or 3♠	

Good 4-card diamond fit, better than a minimum notrump, high honor combination in suit bid.

	SOUTH	NORTH
(13)	1NT	2♣
	2◇	3◇
	3NT	

Minimum notrump with or without a good diamond fit, or a better than minimum notrump without a diamond fit.

	SOUTH	NORTH
(14)	1NT	2♣
	2◇	3◇
	4◇	

Good 4-card diamond fit, maximum notrump, wariness about one or more suits for notrump.

	SOUTH	NORTH
(15)	1NT	2♣
	2♡	3♣ or 3◇
	3♡	

5-card heart suit.

	SOUTH	NORTH
(16)	1NT	2♣
	2♦	2♡
	3♣ or 3♦	

Good 3-card heart fit, maximum no-trump, high honor combination in suit bid, game force if playing strong no-trump, game invitation if playing weak notrump.

	SOUTH	NORTH
(17)	1NT	2♣
	2♦	2♡
	2♠	

Strong notrump: Same as (16) above. *Weak notrump:* See C (3). A rare bid.

	SOUTH	NORTH
(18)	1NT	2♣
	2♠	2NT
	3♣ or 3♦	

Game force, asking if North has 5-card heart suit on the way. South has good 3-card heart support, honor combination in suit bid.

B. *Forcing Stayman versus nonforcing Stayman:*

	SOUTH	NORTH
(1)	1NT	2♣
	2♦	*2♡ or 2♠*
or	1NT	2♣
	2♡	2♠

Strong notrump: one-round force on South. *Weak notrump:* not forcing. South should pass unless he has both a maximum notrump and a good trump fit.

	NORTH	SOUTH
(2)	Pass	1NT
	2♣	2♦
	2♡	
	or 2♠	
or	Pass	1NT
	2♣	2♡
	2♠	

Not forcing. *Strong notrump:* South (a) passes with both a doubleton in support and a minimum notrump, (b) raises partner's suit with tripleton support—to three with a minimum notrump, to four with better or (c) bids two notrump with doubleton support and better than a minimum notrump. *Weak notrump:* Same as if South were dealer—see (1) above.

C. *Stayman with the weak notrump:*

	SOUTH	NORTH
(1)	1NT	2♣

North (a) will play in game or slam, exploring for suit fit, or (b) is looking for better part-score, plans to pass partner's rebid, must be prepared for all of South's three possible rebids.

	SOUTH	NORTH
(2)	1NT	2♣
	2◇	*2♡*

Ordinarily a 5-card suit, but may be only four cards if North is "under pressure."

	SOUTH	NORTH
(3)	1NT	2♣
	2◇	2♡
	2♠	

South has three spades and two hearts, prefers 4-3 spade fit to possible 4-2 heart fit. A rare bid. North must pass.

	SOUTH	NORTH
(4)	1NT	2♣
	2◇	2♡
	3♣ or 3◇	

Maximum notrump, excellent 3-card heart support, strength in suit bid, game invitation.

	SOUTH	NORTH
(5)	1NT	2♣
	2◇	2♡
	3♡	

Pre-emptive, good trump fit.

3. OTHER RESPONSES TO STRONG OPENING NOTRUMP

A. *There is no game when responder has less than a solid 8 points. Otherwise there is no change from the Part I bidding sequences summarized on pages 72-83.*

B. *New and rare Stayman response:*

SOUTH	NORTH
1NT	2♣
2NT	

Maximum notrump, doubleton diamond (thus fear of bidding two diamonds), no 4-card major, running club suit.

4. OTHER RESPONSES TO WEAK OPENING NOTRUMP

	SOUTH	NORTH
(1)	1NT	*Pass*

0-11 points, no preference for a suit contract.

	SOUTH	NORTH
(2)	1NT	*3NT*

12–18 points, no preference for suit contract, no slam interest.

	SOUTH	NORTH	
(3)	1NT	_4♡ or 4♠_	12–18 points (may include distributional points), 6-card or good 5-card suit, no slam interest.

	SOUTH	NORTH	
(4)	1NT	2♡	Game try, excellent heart fit, maximum notrump, strength in suit bid.
	_2♠, 3♣_		
	_or 3◊_		

	SOUTH	NORTH	
(5)	1NT	2♡	Pre-emptive, not invitational.
	_3♡_		

	SOUTH	NORTH	
(6)	1NT	_2NT_	"Unusual notrump," asking partner to bid three of his better minor suit, may be a search for part-score, game or slam.

	NORTH	SOUTH	
(7)	Pass	1NT	Game invitation, exactly 12 points.
	_2NT_		

	NORTH	SOUTH	
(8)	Pass	1NT	5- or 6-card escape suit. South feels this is safer part-score. North must pass.
	2NT	_3♣, 3◊,_	
		_3♡ or 3♠_	

5. COMPETITION AFTER AN OPENING NOTRUMP

A. _"Landy" for takeout:_

	SOUTH	WEST	
(1)	1NT	_2♣_	"Landy," asking for partner's better major suit, has support for both. Usually weaker than 14 points. (May be 15 points of better if hand has no good opening lead, making a double inadvisable.)

	SOUTH	WEST	NORTH	EAST
(2)	1NT	Pass	Pass	*2♣*

"Landy," asking for partner's better major suit, has support for both; rarely 14 points, since there is no "lead problem."

	SOUTH	WEST		
(3)	2NT	*3♣*		

"Landy," asking for partner's better major suit, has support for both; no point requirements, the fewer the points, the more distribution needed.

	SOUTH	WEST	NORTH	EAST
(4)	1NT	2♣	Pass	*2♡*
				or 2♠

Minimum hand, better major, may be 3-card suit.

	SOUTH	WEST	NORTH	EAST
(5)	1NT	2♣	Pass	*3♡*
				or 3♠

About 10 points, game invitation.

	SOUTH	WEST	NORTH	EAST
(6)	1NT	2♣	Pass	*3♣*

Cue-bid, forcing to game, asking West's better major.

	SOUTH	WEST	NORTH	EAST
(7)	1NT	2♣	Pass	*Pass*

Long club suit, no game interest.

	SOUTH	WEST	NORTH	EAST
(8)	1NT	2♣	Pass	*2♢*

Doubletons or worse in the majors, prefers diamonds to clubs, no game interest.

	SOUTH	WEST	NORTH	
(9)	1NT	2♣	*Double*	

Indicates North-South have balance of strength, desire to defend against a doubled contract.

	SOUTH	WEST	NORTH	
(10)	1NT	2♣	*3♣*	

Long club suit, desire to play at three clubs (unless two clubs is a *natural* bid showing a genuine suit; then three clubs is a cue-bid asking for 4-card major).

B. Double

SOUTH WEST
(1) 1NT   *Double*

Essentially a penalty double, with the strength of an opening notrump bid. *After a weak notrump:* 14 points. *After a strong notrump:* 16 points.

SOUTH WEST NORTH EAST
(2) 1NT   Pass   Pass   *Double*

Essentially a penalty double, but may be shaded below opening bid strength.

C. After a Stayman two-club bid:

SOUTH WEST NORTH EAST
(1) 1NT   Pass   2♣   *Double*
   (weak)

14 points or more, no statement about the club suit or major-suit holdings.

SOUTH WEST NORTH EAST
(2) 1NT   Pass   2♣   *Double*
   (strong)

A biddable club suit—informational bid, not a call for partner to act.

SOUTH WEST NORTH EAST
(3) 1NT   Pass   2♣   *3♣*
              (Stayman)

Long club suit, desire to play at three clubs, not forcing.

SOUTH WEST NORTH EAST
(4) 1NT   Pass   2♣   *3♣*
              (natural
              suit bid)

Cue-bid, forcing to game.

SOUTH WEST NORTH EAST
(5) 1NT   Pass   2♣   Pass
   2◊   *Double*

Showing a biddable diamond suit.

6. REDOUBLES

SOUTH WEST NORTH
(1) 1NT   Double   *Redouble*
or NORTH EAST SOUTH WEST
   Pass   Pass   1NT   Double
   Redouble

Strength-showing, good enough to invite game if there had been no double.

	SOUTH	WEST	NORTH	EAST
(2)	1NT	Pass	Pass	Double
	Pass	Pass	*Redouble*	
or	1NT	Pass	Pass	Double
	Redouble			

S.O.S. redouble, asking partner to bid lowest-ranking 4-card suit. Each partner continues bidding his lowest-ranking 4-card suit until 4-3 or 4-4 fit is found.

7. SHOWING A NONVULNERABLE BALANCED HAND OF 15–17 POINTS WHEN PLAYING THE WEAK NOTRUMP

A. *Opener's action:*

	SOUTH	NORTH
(1)	1♣ or 1◊	1♡ or 1♠
	1NT	

15–17 points, balanced hand, stoppers in three suits, would have opened one notrump if vulnerable.

	SOUTH	NORTH
(2)	1♡	1♠
	1NT	

May be (1) above or less than 15 points.

B. *Responses:*

	SOUTH	NORTH
	1♣ or 1◊	1♠
	1NT	?

(1) **2♠**

A desire to play at two spades, 5-card or longer suit.

(2) *2◊ or 2♡*

A two suiter, not forcing on South.

(3) *3♣, 3◊, 3♡*
or 3♠

Natural bid, forcing to game.

(4) *2NT*

Asks opener to bid three notrump with more than a minimum.

	SOUTH	NORTH
(5)	1♣ or 1◊	1♡
	1NT	*2♠*

A reverse, forcing to game, may be 4–4 or 4–5 in the majors.

	SOUTH	NORTH	
(6)	1♣ or 1◇	1♡ or 1♠	Stayman, game interest.
	1NT	2♣	

C. *Opener's replies to Stayman—with a minimum hand:*

	SOUTH	NORTH
	1♣ or 1◇	1♠
	1NT	2♣
	?	

(1)	2♡	Biddable 4-card heart holding.
(2)	2♠	No biddable 4-card heart holding, but a 3-card spade suit (would have raised immediately with four spades).
(3)	2◇	Neither biddable 4-card heart suit nor 3-card spade support.

D. *Opener's replies to Stayman—with better than a minimum hand:*

	SOUTH	NORTH
	1♣ or 1◇	1♠
	1NT	2♣
	?	

(1)	3♡	Biddable 4-card heart holding.
(2)	3♠	No biddable 4-card heart holding, but a 3-card spade suit.
(3)	3♣ or 3◇	Neither a biddable 4-card heart suit nor 3-card spade support, side strength in the minor bid.
(4)	2NT	Same as (3) but no preference between the minors.

	SOUTH	NORTH	
(5)	1♣ or 1◇	1♡	Four spades; forces the bidding to two notrump or higher, hence shows better than a minimum.
	1NT	2♣	
	2♠		

E. *Responses to "extended" Stayman:*

SOUTH	NORTH	
1♡	1♠	Natural bid, but shows less
1NT	2♣	than 15 points. (Any other re-
2♡ or 2♠		bid shows a hand in the 15-to-17-point range.)

8. BIGGER HANDS THAN THE STRONG NOTRUMP (SAME MEANING WHETHER VULNERABLE OR NONVULNERABLE)

A. *Showing a balanced hand of more than 17 points but less than a good 20:*

SOUTH	NORTH	
1♣	1◊, 1♡ or 1♠	18 to 20– points, stoppers in
2NT		all but partner's suit, balanced hand.

B. *When playing weak two-bids—with strong or weak notrump:*

	OPENER	
(1)	*2NT*	20–22 points, balanced hand, stoppers in all four suits.

	SOUTH	NORTH	
(2)	2♣	2◊, 2♡ or 2♠	23–24 points, balanced hand,
	2NT		stoppers in all four suits.

	OPENER	
(3)	*3NT*	25–26 points, balanced hand, stoppers in all four suits.

	SOUTH	NORTH	
(4)	2♣	2◊, 2♡ or 2♠	27–28 points, balanced hand,
	3NT		stoppers in all four suits.

9. NONVULNERABLE NOTRUMP OVERCALL

A. *May be standard:*

EAST	SOUTH	
1♣, 1◊,	*1NT*	16–18 points, stoppers in three
1♡ or 1♠		suits including opponent's (double stopper if only 16 points).

B. May be tactical:

EAST	SOUTH		
(1) 1♣, 1◇,	*1NT*		
1♡ or 1♠			

Strong 6- or 7-card minor suit, virtually no side values.

EAST	SOUTH	WEST	NORTH
(2) 1♣, 1◇,	1NT	Pass	*2♣*
1♡ or 1♠			

Stayman, but asking not for majors but whether North has a standard or tactical no-trump.

EAST	SOUTH	WEST	NORTH
(3) 1♣, 1◇,	1NT	Pass	2♣
1♡ or 1♠			
Pass	*2NT*		

Confirms 16-to-18-point no-trump.

EAST	SOUTH	WEST	NORTH
(4) 1♣, 1◇,	1NT	Pass	2♣
1♡ or 1♠			
Pass	*2◇, 3♣*		
	or 3◇		

Tactical notrump based on suit bid.

10. TWO DIAMONDS OVER ONE NOTRUMP FOR MINORS

A. The basic bid:

SOUTH	NORTH
1NT	*2◇*

11 points minimum (14 if opposite weak notrump), singleton or void, five cards in at least one minor, no interest in South's major-suit *length;* South is requested to describe his major-suit *stoppers.*

B. Opener's reply:

SOUTH	NORTH
(1) 1NT	2◇
2♡ or 2♠	

Good stopper (minimum of Q 10 x) in major bid, lacks a good stopper in the other major.

SOUTH	NORTH
(2) 1NT	2◇
2NT	

Good stoppers (minimum of Q 10 x) in both majors.

	SOUTH	NORTH
(3)	1NT	2♢
	_3♣ or 3♢_	

No good major-suit stopper, long and strong in minor bid. (Applicable only after weak notrump; impossible bid after strong notrump.)

C. Responder's rebid:

	SOUTH	NORTH
(1)	1NT	2♢
	2♡ or 2♠	_3NT_

Short in South's major. Notrump therefore best spot. South is barred from further action.

	SOUTH	NORTH
(2)	1NT	2♢
	2♡ or 2♠	_3♣ or 3♢_

Short in the unbid major. Showing better minor. Asks if South fits this suit.

	SOUTH	NORTH
(3)	1NT	2♢
	2♡ or 2♠	_2NT_

Some length or a stopper in the unbid major, but short in a minor. Asks about South's minor suits.

	SOUTH	NORTH
(4)	1NT	2♢
	2♡	_2♠_

Good spade stopper, short in a minor. Asks about South's minor suits.

	SOUTH	NORTH
(5)	1NT	2♢
	2NT	_3♣ or 3♢_

North's better minor, asks if South has a stopper in the other minor (South should assume for the moment that this is North's short suit).

D. Opener's third bid:

	SOUTH	NORTH
(1)	1NT	2♢
	2♠	2NT
	_3♣_	

Very good clubs in a maximum hand. Having already denied a heart stopper South cannot also lack diamond stopper, therefore an encouraging bid.

	SOUTH	NORTH
(2)	1NT	2♢
	2♠	2NT
	_3NT_	

Stoppers in both minors, but near minimum hand and/or fit.

	SOUTH	NORTH	
(3)	1NT	2◇	Cue-bidding an ace, suggesting a club slam by inference.
	2♡	3♣	
	3◇ or 3♡		

	SOUTH	NORTH	
(4)	1NT	2◇	No ace to cue-bid, but a maximum notrump and fit.
	2♡	3♣	
	5♣		

	SOUTH	NORTH	
(5)	1NT	2◇	No ace to cue-bid, partial spade stopper, suggesting three notrump as best contract.
	2♡	3♣	
	3NT		

	SOUTH	NORTH	
(6)	1NT	2◇	No ace to cue-bid, no partial spade stopper, a minimum notrump and/or fit.
	2♡	3♣	
	4♣		

	SOUTH	NORTH	
(7)	1NT	2◇	Good diamond stopper, warning against going further.
	2NT	3♣	
	3NT		

E. Advanced use of two-diamond convention:

	SOUTH	NORTH	
(1)	1NT	*2◇*	May have good 5-card major and only 4-card minor.

	SOUTH	NORTH	
(2)	1NT	2◇	Wants to play there. Confirms 5-card or longer major suit; South's response disappointing for slam purposes.
	2♡, 2♠	*4♡ or 4♠*	
	or 2NT		

	SOUTH	NORTH	
(3)	1NT	2◇	Shows good 5-card major suit, asks South for more information, slam is still a possibility.
	2♡	*2♠ or 3♡*	
or	1NT	2◇	
	2♠ or 2NT	*3♡ or 3♠*	

11. SLAM-BIDDING TECHNIQUES

A. Stayman to uncover suit fits:

SOUTH	NORTH	
1NT	2♣	Asking for more information, hoping
2◇	*3♣ or 3◇*	to find 4–4 fit in bid minor.

B. Implied fit or indirect raise:

	SOUTH	NORTH	
(1)	1NT	2♣	Good 4-card diamond fit, heart
	2◇	3◇	strength, better than a minimum no-
	3♡		trump.

	SOUTH	NORTH	
(2)	1NT	3♡	Confirms heart fit, shows high spade
	3♠		honor, better than a minimum no-
			trump.

C. Cue-bidding after trump suit is agreed:

	SOUTH	NORTH	
(1)	1NT	2♣	Diamonds is the trump suit, so this
	2◇	3◇	shows spade ace.
	3♡	*3♠*	

	SOUTH	NORTH	
(2)	1NT	3♡	Hearts are agreed upon by inference,
	3♠	*4◇*	so this shows diamond ace (and de-
			nies club ace).

D. Exploring the fourth suit:

	SOUTH	NORTH	
(1)	1NT	3♡	South does not have second-round
	4◇	5♣	control of the fourth suit, spades.
	5♡		

	SOUTH	NORTH	
(2)	1NT	3♡	Shows K x of the fourth suit, spades.
	4◇	5♣	
	5NT		

	SOUTH	NORTH
(3)	1NT	3♡
	4◇	5♣
	6♡	

Shows K Q of the fourth suit, spades.

	SOUTH	NORTH
(4)	1NT	3♡
	4◇	5♣
	5♠	

Shows ace of fourth suit, spades.

12. ACE–COUNTING CONVENTIONS

A. Blackwood versus Gerber:

	SOUTH	NORTH
(1)	1NT	2♣
	2♠	*4♣*

Gerber, ace-asking, since suit is agreed upon by inference.

	SOUTH	NORTH
(2)	1NT	3♠
	4♠	*4NT*

Blackwood, ace-asking, since suit has been agreed upon and four clubs (Gerber) is not available.

	SOUTH	NORTH
(3)	1NT	3♠
	3NT	*4NT*

Notrump raise, slam suggestion; not ace-asking, as four clubs was available.

B. Modified Roman responses for aces:

	BLACKWOOD		GERBER		
	SOUTH	NORTH	SOUTH	NORTH	
	4NT	?	4♣	?	
(1)		*5♣*		*4◇*	No or three aces.
(2)		*5◇*		*4♡*	One or four aces.
(3)		*5♡*		*4♠*	Two aces.

C. Modified Roman responses for kings:

BLACKWOOD		GERBER	
SOUTH	NORTH	SOUTH	NORTH
4NT	5 in suit	4♣	4 in suit
5NT	?	5♣	?

(1)   6♣   5◊   No or three kings (not all in bid suits).

(2)   6◊   5♡   One king in unbid suit or four kings.

(3)   6♡   5♠   One king in bid suit.

(4)   6♠   5NT   Two kings, but not both in bid suits.

(5)   6NT   6♣   Two kings, both in bid suits.

(6)   7♣   6◊   Three kings, all in bid suits.

13. GRAND-SLAM FORCES

A. Standard:

SOUTH	NORTH
1NT	3♡
3♠	4◊
5♣	5NT

Asking South to bid seven hearts if he has two of the three top hearts.

B. After Blackwood:

SOUTH	NORTH
1♡	3 ♡
4NT	5 ◊
6♣ or 6◊	

Asking North to bid seven hearts if he has two of the top three hearts.